The Life of Allie Rae Setterington Williams

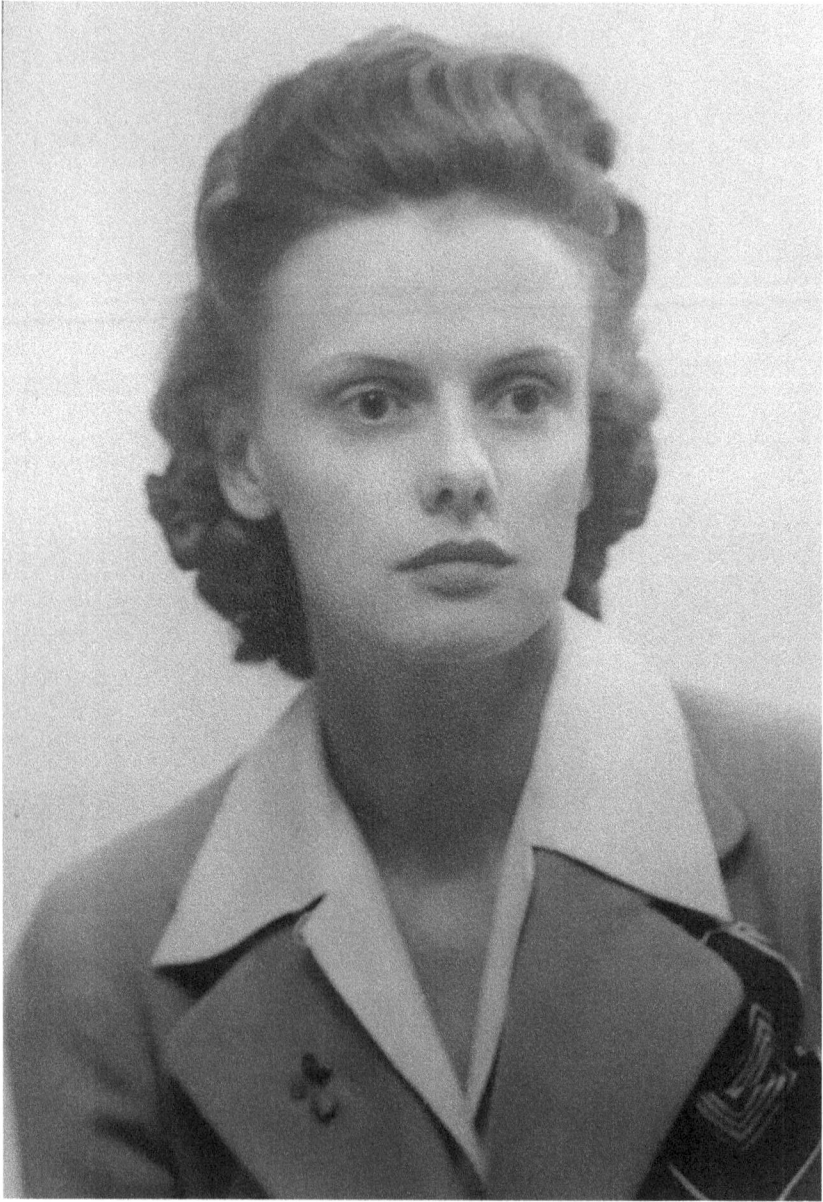

The Life of Allie Rae Setterington Williams

Contributions by

Allie Rae Setterington Williams
Anne Lyon
Rebekah Anderson
Harold Williams

WAKING LION PRESS

ISBN 978-1-4341-0426-7

Published by Waking Lion Press, an imprint of The Editorium

Waking Lion Press™, the Waking Lion Press logo, and The Editorium™ are trademarks of The Editorium, LLC

The Editorium, LLC
West Jordan, UT 84081-6132
wakinglionpress.com
wakinglion@editorium.com

CONTENTS

Personal History of Allie Rae Setterington Williams

I was born in Calgary, Alberta, Canada, on a cold blustery Good Friday morning, March 25th, 1921. My Mother often said in later years that I got my "sunny" disposition from that cold and windy day??? I was born in our home, which then was 230 12th Avenue West. I believe my grandparents (my Father's parents) were visiting our home at that time and had the privilege of naming me after their baby daughter who died when only a few days old. I always thought that was pretty nice, and I felt honored, altho to this day I don't care much for my name.

I was the second girl and middle child in our family. My Mother was Mabel Alice Rogers Setterington of Detroit, Michigan, and my Father was Harold Aubrey Setterington of Leamington, Ontario. Helen Ruth was three years older than I, then came Jack Leland, my only brother, who was about eighteen months older. My two younger sisters, Josephine Mable and Geraldine Audrey, were three and six years younger consecutively.

My early recollections were of our home on 12th avenue. It was a nice, comfortable home with lots of pretty flowers in our yard. I'm sure that Mother planted them all and cared for them too. We had a walk from the sidewalk to our front porch made out of lengths of wood raised up from the ground. So many many things were lost between those boards. I often think what fun to go back now and look beneath to find our childish treasures. But of course that is impossible, as the house has long since been removed and the lot turned over to a car dealership.

Our yard was fenced in, and it was the gathering place for all our friends. Mother always kept us close to home but welcomed the neighborhood children in to play. So with five children plus many others, you

Rae and her older sister, Ruth, "Canadian Girls in Training" (CGIT). Rae was Miss Yukon; Ruth was Miss Quebec. Note the board steps and sidewalk.

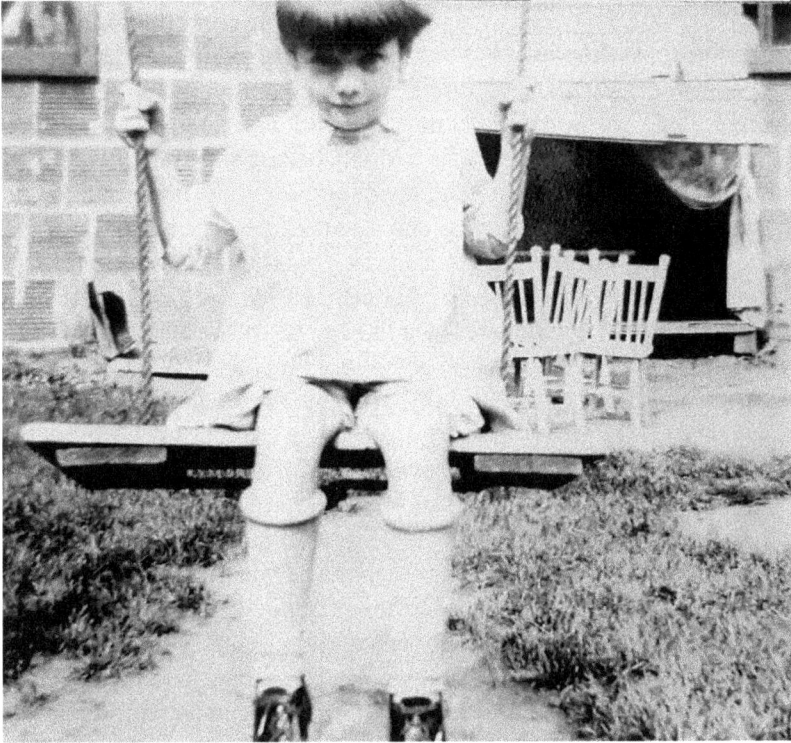

Five-year-old Rae swinging in front of the piano-box playhouse. Note the curtains on the playhouse.

can imagine the happy laughter that came forth many an evening just before sunset. There we learned to ride our bikes by holding on to the fence all around the back yard. We took turns, and finally as we grew more adept we were allowed to venture outside our yard. My first bike cost $18.00, and it was maroon. I was so proud of it. My brother Jack had a bike too, so we had to share with the others in our family.

I believe my earliest recollections are when I was four or five. We had a big piano box in our back yard which we had fixed up to be our playhouse. It was fun playing in it, and I remember Mother gave us old curtains to put on the make-believe windows. One day I got some matches from the house and set the curtains on fire??? Needless to say, not only the curtains were destroyed but the playhouse went too.

I suppose I got a spanking for it, but I can't remember that part of the story. I m sure when asked about the accident I probably lied. We also had a swing in the back yard, and I have a picture somewhere of me swinging in it. We could play under our back porch too, because there is where I made all my mud pies with my baking set. Mother would let me turn on the hose and make lots of mud for my pies and cakes. We would decorate them with grass and weeds and set them out in the sun to bake. When it came time to clean up, my friends *always* had to go home. I remember mostly Bert and Edward Taylor were the ones to help me bake. They were twin boys who lived up in the next block and were really my brother's friends. We remained friends for years and years. They would call my Mother and Dad Aunt Mabel and Uncle Harold. We were to call their parents aunt and uncle too, but I don't think we did too much, altho we surely loved them lots. Probably the happiest days of the summer was when we were allowed to go under the hose. We couldn't get on our bathing suits fast enough. We played for hours chasing each other thru the hose. What fun it was! I also have pictures of us in our bathing suits. How strange they look to us now.

I remember so well our front yard and the fence which kept us in. We had a gate, and I would swing on the gate back and forth. When people came by and spoke, I would stick my tongue out, and someone told Mother it almost covered my whole face? Can you imagine? About that time Gerrie was born, and my dad took us to the hospital to see her. What a thrill. I remember as tho it was yesterday. She had a little brown mole on her wrist. Our neighbor across the street, Mrs. Aull, used to tease me and call across the street she was coming over to steal the baby. I didn't like that one bit and used to call back some words that meant "Shut up, Mrs. Aull." It sounded like shup up Aull. Funny that's still in my mind.

Starting school was a thrilling experience, altho I was frightened. We attended Haultain school, which was just two blocks away. We walked it easily and would come home for lunch. Mrs. Glassford was my first teacher. Mondays Mother always had the washing machine going, and the house would smell of soapy water and bluing. The floors were always covered with newspapers. I went to that school for six years and had all old-maid teachers. Only one was married, and she was a widow. We had good times there, and I remember my friends & their names and where they lived. Zillah Leon was my first friend, and we were often

Jo, Ruth, Jack, Gerrie, and Rae, ready to run through the hose.

mistaken for sisters. Betty Hayden was another friend who lived up the street in the Barnhart apts. That was my first experience of apt. houses, and from then on I've always wanted to live in an apt. My best girlhood friend was Marjorie Kerr, who lived up on fourth street in an upstairs apt. We were friends for years and years. In fact, I introduced her to her first boyfriend, who later became her husband. Her Father, Mr. Kerr, was such a kind, gentle man. He was in poor health due to working years in the coal mine up around Rocky Mountain House. My Dad gave him a job and an apt. rent free for taking care of the building. He seemed so happy with the work. Marjorie was always ashamed of where they lived. As we grew up and had boyfriends and dates, she would always want to spend the night at our house so her date wouldn't see where she lived. I felt sorry for her and always complied with her wishes. In our teens, early teens that is, we wanted to be chorus girls and run away to New York city. We said we would just as soon as we were 18 yrs old. Can you imagine? We practiced many an hour in our basement learning to tap dance. Sometimes we'd spend Friday nights at each others' house. Her mother always brought our breakfast to bed. What a treat. How we looked forward to that. On Saturdays we would go to the show, then later go up to her apt for a snack before I had to catch the bus for home. Those were happy, wonderful years together. One special weekend her parents took us to Banff for the day. For the occasion we bought green and white striped bicycle shorts and white shoes. For days we prayed the weather would be nice. It was, and that was one of the happiest days we ever spent together. We were up hours ahead of time so we'd be certain to be ready when her folks came for us. We spent almost the whole day in the pool at Banff. When it came time to go home, I remember Marjorie cried almost the whole way home. She was afraid she'd never get back up there again. I don't remember if she ever did. As I recall, she had a terrible crush on my brother, Jack. She would go on for hours about him. One night when she was spending the night, Jack hid under our bed, and I got her talking about him. She went on and on, and all the time he was listening. When he came out from under the bed, she nearly died from embarrassment. Wasn't that a horrible trick to play on her? Now I'm so ashamed, but then I thought it was so funny.

During those years in school, my Mother was famous for the school's candy sales. Mother was known far and wide for her marvelous home-made candy. They always called on her to supply lots of her fudge and other kinds of candy for the sale. Because of her great ability, the sales were always a huge success. We were so proud of Mother. As I recall, Mother's whole life was centered around her family. For all the many school plays, etc., Mother made all our costumes. Years later we found our paper costumes packed away in her old trunk in the basement. I was a crocus and Ruth was a rose. What beautiful costumes we had. She kept all the mementoes from our childhood years: Jack's boy scout socks, our Hallowe'en costumes she made for us, papers we brought home from school. What marvelous times I had years later going thru the trunks and reminiscing. She kept our baby jewelry, and only when we left home did she give them to us. I got my baby ring, bracelet, and necklace to give to my own children when they came along.

One of the most important events was the time my Dad learned to drive. He must have been in his early forties. He bought a 1930 Hudson. It was his pride and joy. He took lessons from the salesman and after much practice at long last learned to drive. I recall the first time he took us all out, when it came time to pull in the driveway he went around the block eighteen times before he had enough nerve to pull across the street into our drive. But it wasn't long before he became a very good driver. In the summer of 1930 he took his three oldest children Ruth, Jack, and myself along with his very good friend Ned Swanson on a wonderful trip east to visit his parents in Leamington, Ontario, and my great Aunt Allie in St. Mary's, Ontario, and Mother's sister and her husband and her Mother in Detroit, Mich. That was Aunt Maude, Uncle Tommie, and Grandmother Rogers. What a grand trip it was down and back. I have the original diary in my possession. In those years there were many trips east on the train. Mother took the two youngest once, and that was Jo and Gerrie. Before that, she took Ruth back east when she was just a baby. My Dad took Jo and I on the train once. Another time he took Jo and Gerrie. Then when his Father died, he went back to settle the estate and clear things up for my grandmother.

I'll talk later about the trips east and how much they meant to us. Right now I want to remember the years growing up and of events at school.

When I was about 10 or 11, we girls had our tonsils out in the Western Nursing home just a few blocks from our house. It was kept a secret, I suppose so we wouldn't worry about it. I remember I wasn't told until the morning we left for the hospital. When Mother told me, I cried

Rae, about 1936, in a Halloween costume for a dance at Western Canada High School. On the back of this picture, Rae wrote, "I was so nervous I wished the school would burn down. It did, one week later."

Harold Aubrey Setterington with Ruth, Jack, Jo, and Rae, and Harold's good friend Ned Swanson, in front of Harold's 1930 Hudson.

and carried on something terrible. I can see now the wisdom in not letting me know ahead of time. It was just a small nursing home, and quite private. We all sat on the front porch waiting our turn. Ruth went first and then Gerrie. They shared a room together at the front, just off the porch. When it came my turn, I remember walking into the operating room and saying it looked just like we were going to hell. What a remark. Well, I was so terrified I suppose that was the only thing I could think of. I'm sure I thought I would die. We finally all came thru it okay, and when I awoke there was Jo in a bed next to me. How my throat hurt, and how good chipped ice tasted when the nurse brought it to us. Jack and his friends would come over each day and call to us thru the window. It was fun having so much attention. After we went home, Mother would fix us the most delicious strawberry drink made from fresh berries. I can taste it still after over 40 years. Gerrie was the only one who had any after-effects, and one night she started to hemorrhage. The doctor came and swabbed her throat to stop the bleeding. I can still hear her screaming as I ran down the street away from the house.

We lived in our house until I was 13 years old, and they were such happy years. In 1930, or thereabouts I think, my grandparents came out for a visit. I recall playing in the living room under the quilting frame and having such fun. In the mornings we would climb in bed with our grandparents and jump and scream and play with them. I suppose as grandparents they thought that was great sport. I was always my grandmother's favorite, and now I realize it was due to the fact that I was named after their baby girl who died. It was always my good fortune to sleep with my grandmother whenever we went east. I can remember the room with the "pot" under the bed. She didn't have inside plumbing in those days. They had a beautiful big house on a corner lot with a huge porch surrounding part of the house. Their front parlor was always closed with the blinds down except when "company" came. How I wish now that I could go back and see that home again and be able to walk thru the rooms once more. The floors were of inlaid hardwood and very beautiful, I remember. Across the street was the Heinz factory, and at noon and mornings and late afternoon, they would blow the whistle for the benefit of the workers. It was so loud you could hear it for miles. It sent a chill thru us until we got used to it. My cousin Beth Setterington lived up the street about two blocks, and she and I would play together when we weren't swimming. She was Bill Setterington's daughter. Her stepmother was Flossie. Flossie still lives in that big, red brick home alone. Our cousins Mary and Francis Curtis lived just across the street at the Curtis farm. We would visit there too, I recall. They were several years older than we were. They both worked in the factory. One year they had a Setterington reunion, and we all attended. All I remember about it was all the old people my Dad seemed to know. It was fun for him, but we soon tired of it.

Most of our time was spent swimming in Lake Erie, which was just straight down the road from my grandparents' home. It was quite a long walk, but we never minded too much as it meant fun for us when we reached the lake. Leamington was a beautiful old town, and one of the streets was named after my great-grandfather. My Dad spent most of his time visiting with the older members of the family and with cousins, old friends, etc. From there we always returned to Detroit, where we finished up our holidays before starting for home. We thought Detroit was about the grandest city in the world. Aunt Maude and Uncle Tommie always made a big fuss over us and treated us royally and took us to so many marvelous places. It was such a thrill to go downtown and see the huge skyscrapers and watch the boats come down the Detroit river.

We used to wonder why Mother ever left that marvelous place to travel west to Calgary. Of course, those years we saw things thru children's eyes. It's far different as seen years and years later. Now, to me, Detroit is just a huge, noisy, and dirty city. I would never choose to live there.

One of my outstanding memories of the years on 12th avenue was my very special celebration for my birthdays. My Dad took me for lunch in the Palliser Hotel, which was then the finest hotel in the city. I took a note to school on that special day asking to let me out early in order to have lunch with my Dad. I would race home and change into my Sunday clothes (my best), then walk as fast as I could to his office, which was downtown on 8th avenue. It wasn't too far, so it didn't take me long. A fellow businessman in the same office always came with us. I can't remember his name now, but he always smoked a cigar. He was a tall, thin man with gray hair, and very handsome, I thought. Each year he gave me a box of Picardy's chocolates. On the top of the box was a verse titled "Out Where the West Begins." I wish that I could recite it now, but I can't.[1] Mother remarked how beautiful it was. Most of the time I would be early getting to my Dad's office, so he always invited me into his office where the huge vault was kept. He would open it and show beautiful jewelry that belonged to some of his clients. My Dad

---

1. Out where the handclasp's a little stronger,
Out where the smile dwells a little longer,
That's where the West begins;
Out where the sun is a little brighter,
Where the snows that fall are a trifle whiter,
Where the bonds of home are a wee bit tighter,
That's where the West begins.

Out where the skies are a trifle bluer,
Out where friendship's a little truer,
That's where the West begins;
Out where a fresher breeze is blowing,
Where there's laughter in every streamlet flowing,
Where there's more of reaping and less of sowing,
That's where the West begins;

Out where the world is in the making,
Where fewer hearts in despair are aching,
That's where the West begins;
Where there's more of singing and less of sighing,
Where there's more of giving and less of buying,
And a man makes friends without half trying—
That's where the West begins.

—Arthur Chapman

Jack, Rae, and Jo at Lake Erie, Leamington, Ontario.

was an estates manager. I loved looking at everything, and as a child I was very impressed. He always wanted me to do a little dance for him, and altho I hated doing it, I would just to please him. I was always so crazy about him and would do anything he asked me to. I don't know if he ever took Jack or my sisters out to lunch on their birthdays. I've often wondered since why I was the lucky one.

As I was growing up on 12th avenue, I recall we always had a maid to help Mother with the work. She usually had a room someplace where she stayed overnight, but she worked at our house during the day except on Thurs. afternoons, which was her day off. We had many, many different ones, as none of them seemed to stay very long. One in particular stayed with us for nine years. She was from Edinburgh, Scotland, and her name was Effie Rankin. We liked her especially well. Another one was Minnie Jutie, a girl from Finland. She worked in our home two different times. Now from this you might think we were rich. Well, as a child I used to think that we were, but as I look back I know that we weren't. Mother had very poor health those years after Jo was born, and with four small children she needed help with the housework. After Jo was born, Mother had Phlebitis and was confined to bed for 6 months. Of course I don't remember that as I was only 3, but Mother talked about it.

One year when I was 5, our family rented a huge home in Victoria, BC, where we spent one summer. It was marvelous, as I recall, and swimming in the Pacific ocean was great fun. That was the year that the hit song "Valencia" came out, and my Dad travelled as far away as Seattle just to buy the record. I have several pictures taken of our family while on the coast. One of my favorites is of my Dad with we four children walking along the beach. Gerrie wasn't born then. I don't suppose there ever was a Dad who loved his family more. Dad was so very, very proud of us as long as I can remember. Many is the night he got us washed and ready for bed. He never took a trip without at least one or two or three of us going along. He always wanted to show us off. Even after we were grown up.

My Dad wrote a poem about us when we were all small. It seemed he had a cousin named Addie who wrote one about her son. Not to be outdone, my grandmother insisted he write one of his family. He spent every waking minute for the next few days composing it, and here it

The Palliser Hotel.

Ruth, Minnie Jutie (maid), Rae, and Jo.

is. I want all of our children to have a copy of it and to hand down to their children too. I called it "Our Family."

> *Now Addie my dear*
> *Though you're old and queer*
> *Don't try to hand us some taffy*
> *We hope you are right*
> *That the boys are bright*
> *But you must be a little bit daffy.*
>
> *Now Addie, you beauty*
> *You've failed in your duty*
> *As your offspring was only one son*

Jo, Harold, Rae, Jack, and Ruth at the beach on the Pacific Ocean.

You're a good little poet
And there's many that know it
But you should have done better than one.

Your grandchildren too
Are you know very few
So thinks, perhaps, their Daddy
They now have you beat
So let them repeat
For they may want one to call Addie.

Now beautiful Addie
You know to be Daddy
Is the ambition of nearly all men
Leave the children alone
Or you'll surely atone
Because they may want to have ten.

Just a little advice
I'll not give it twice

You know that large families are few
So why tell your daughter
You think that she otter
Take any advice from you.

We 've been married ten years
And have gone thru the fears
Of raising the ones we adore
Some people have one
While others have none
And we pity those who'd like more.

Our children are five
And all much alive
And each worth their weight in gold
We'd like to have eight
But got started too late
And now we are getting too old.

Our first girl was Ruth
And to tell you the truth
My head almost burst with her beauty
She's a very smart lass
At the top of her class
And to keep her to school is our duty.

Jack the second a boy
Afforded much joy
As he had a head like a poet
He soon will be eight
Unless decreed by fate
Make his mark in this world and you'll know it.

Our third Allie Rae
Was by far and away
The cleverest of all five
She has wit and grace
And beauty of face
And on deviltry seems to thrive.

Jo the fourth is a girl
Whose hair has the curl

And whose looks to possess you'd be glad
She is far from a mute
And oh so cute
And looks just like her Dad.

Our fifth named Gerrie
Then decided to tarry.
From raising more than five
She's only a baby
And her beauty maybe
Is possessed by no other alive.

With a family so nifty
Who would not feel thrifty
Tho at times they will make you feel sad
We doubt if there ever
Were children so clever
With such a good looking Mother and Dad.

Though your legs are bowed
But are not pigeon-toed
You're one cousin I've always adored
If you ever come west
We will give you a nest
And see that you get your board.

I recall one summer we rented a cottage at Sylvan Lake for two weeks. We arrived after dark, and after looking for some time we finally spied a building which Daddy mistook for the garage??? As it turned out, it was the house. What a shocker that was. No conveniences at all, and so dirty, too. Well, we spent almost two weeks, and every one of the children got sick. With Mother's excellent care we recovered, with the exception of me. Mother took me home on the train. Dr. Bouck came out to the house to see me, and after taking a few blood samples, etc., he could find nothing wrong. But miraculously I soon recovered and was back to normal. The conclusion they came to was the fact that I was just "homesick". And that certainly told them and me a great deal about myself and of how my future would affect me in my many years of moving after I was married. It was about that time on my way home by

Home in Rideau Park, where Rae lived until she got married.

train that I began seriously to think about becoming a nurse. A desire I kept for years and years, after which, I'm sorry to say, never materialized.

In Sept. the year that I was 13, we bought our home in Rideau Park, and that was so exciting. It was a 6 bedroom home with a huge yard. Daddy had a lot of remodeling done before we moved in, such as making an extra bedroom by raising the back roof, new light fixtures, painting the exterior, etc. It was just beautiful, and Mother especially was so proud of it. She hired a landscape artist, and he planned and planted our yard. Dad bought the next door lot, where for several years we raised potatoes. After, we planted a lawn plus fruit trees and added a summer house, too, which made it beautiful. We were happy in our home, and for years after and all the time we owned it, we would invite our friends to come and visit. We were within walking distance of Rideau Junior high school, and that is where we attended. Later, during our high school years, we attended Western Canada high school on 17th ave.

When I was 17 years old, I attended St Joseph's Convent in Red Deer. It was a Catholic school, and there I made lasting friendships. It was a marvelous two years, and of course while there I had the very strong desire to become a Catholic and later a nun. Of course, this upset my parents very much, and in the spring of 1939 this was the real reason for not being able to finish my studies there. At the time I thought it was a real tragedy, but in the years to come I could see the blessings from it. But at the time I didn't have the wisdom that comes with age. However, the separation from the convent didn't change the affection I had for my dear friend Sr. Denise, who was then and still is my loyal friend.

While I attended the convent, I was allowed to go home about once a month or every six weeks. What a treat to get some really good homecooked meals and to be with my friends and not have to go to bed and get up at a fixed time every day. It was a thrill each time we went home, and of course I always had lots of tales to relate about life in a convent. One special weekend Mother planned a hay ride party for Jack and I and our friends. Daddy rented a sled a driver and a team of horses, and after we all climbed aboard, we rode all over the outskirts of Calgary in the moonlight with the snow glistening. I can still picture how beautiful it was. When we arrived back home, Mother had hot chocolate and doughnuts ready for us. Then we rolled back the rugs and danced. What a marvelous time we had. Another time I was allowed to come home for a very special occasion. Ruth's 21st birthday, held at the Renfrew Club. It was a very swish affair with formals, music, and all that goes with it. Mother and Daddy and friends of theirs were the chaperones. We had a great time dancing to such tunes as The Lambeth Walk, In the Mood, etc.

Mother always packed me a box of food to take back up to the convent with me. After all my complaining about the food, she took pity on me. I always had peanut butter cookies and fudge. I'm sure there were other things too, but those were my favorites. One time I sneaked a can of condensed milk to take back. I had asked Mother if I could have it, and she said no. I took it anyway. What a kid I was. I wouldn't do that now.

Well, I spent two years there, and they were lovely years. Now this past summer I learned that they are to tear down the convent and replace it with a much smaller building. Just big enough to house the sisters who are left. I'm happy that I could visit it once more.

When I was eighteen, I had to have my appendix out, so that was the end of my convent days. After the surgery, the doctor advised Mother not to let me return. I spent the remainder of the school year attending Mount Royal college in Calgary. I lost so many credits that year that that was the main reason for never finishing high school at that time. No matter how many letters Sr. Denise wrote to Mother, Mother wouldn't

Harold and Mabel, 1936.

change her mind about my returning to the convent. I suppose that was my first really bitter disappointment. However, I did get to go back for visits on the weekend, and that was marvelous to be with all the girls again and to continue my talks with Sr. Denise. And so after all these years (1937–1977), we are still good friends and keep in touch. That was a very special time of my life. I feel so fortunate to have experienced it.

These past ten years or so there have been no boarders or students at the convent. Now it's just a home for the nuns who are left. I'm sure as they rattle around in those empty halls and rooms, memories of years gone by come flooding back and give the sisters a feeling of sadness and loneliness. I felt it when I was there recently, and so I could share empathy with them. I could empathize with them.

We had many marvelous trips east with our parents. The last one we took together was in 1939. But before that in 1936 or 1937, we drove to Spokane, Wash., over the newly opened Logan Pass in Glacier National Park in Montana. What a scary road that was for us. We had car trouble, and Dad was so nervous driving over those high roads. The road was just wide enough for two cars to pass most of the time. It took eighteen miles to climb to the summit, and only four to get back down. What a trip. By the time we got off it, we were all nervous wrecks. On our return trip, we came home thru British Columbia. We did have a fun time in Spokane, tho, and went swimming every day in one of the many public pools.

Our trip east in 1939 was a fun trip like all the others. While in Detroit we stayed with Mother's old friend Vera Cook. They took us to dinner in the very swank Yacht Club to which they belonged. We were so impressed with such lush surroundings and to see all the yachts moored at the docks. There were eighteen of them altogether, and it was a fun time. I recall Harold Crook (Vera's adopted son) took me to the club and home in his car. Was I ever on my best behaviour. When he offered me a cigarette, I declined and said I'd have one later???? I didn't even smoke. But here I was trying to act so mature. He must have guessed the truth and smiled to himself. We spent some time in St. Marys, where Aunt Maude and uncle Tommie had taken over Aunt Allie's hotel. By this time Aunt Allie was getting on in years but was still and always the same beautiful person. She and I were always the best of friends, and she took me shopping to a jewelry store where she bought me a lovely gold locket with a tiny blue center. I could open

Friend and Rae at the convent.

it up and put pictures on either side. I can still picture it in my mind, altho it has long since been gone. Dear Aunt Allie, how I did love her. We went to Leamington that summer too. That was our last trip east as a family. That was the year we drove our brand new 1939 Chrysler. Jack bought it in Detroit that spring.

As I look back over the years, I recall happy happy times we had together as a family doing fun things. And during my whole life spent at home I *always* had a feeling of security as tho nothing bad could ever happen to me. I had such faith in my Father and Mother and in our home. What marvelous years they were while I was growing up. Truly happy, wonderful years.

As we grew up in our home, we never had the gospel or any knowledge of it, but we did have a little religion training. While we were quite young, we attended the First Baptist church on 4th st., and then later after they built the Presbyterian church on 2d st., we went there to Mission Band (which we hated) on Sat. PM. Sunday School and church on Sunday. After we moved to Rideau Park, we changed our membership to Central United church, which was located downtown. And there we stayed the remainder of our youth. It was a lovely, big church, and one of the most prosperous in Calgary. It was a Methodist church. I enjoyed going there, and we had some fun times over the years. I was baptized when I was sixteen years old. It was during the holidays while I was home for Christmas. Consenting to it was the only way I could return to the convent. Because it was during that holiday that I informed my Mother that I wanted to become a Catholic and later a nun. Can you imagine the concern of my parents? Well!? Believe me, Mother did everything in her power to keep me from making such a huge mistake. Now I look back and see the wisdom in her decision, but at the time I was heartbroken.

During the time after I was out of school and before I was married, I worked at several different jobs, one of which was for two dentists. It was my favorite work, and I loved it. I stayed with them two years, then began work at Henry Birks and Sons, which was a very exclusive jewelry store. That was a fun time, and I had many good times while there.

I should say that during my working years was the time of the second world war, and we had many, many servicemen stationed in Calgary. Girls didn't lack for dates, and I had my share of them. I got acquainted and went with boys from all over the country. Some were exceptionally

Rae's Aunt Allie.

Front row: *Ruth, Jack, Rae, Jo.* Back row: *Maid, Mabel, Harold.*

well behaved, while others were not. It wasn't difficult to tell the differ-ence. Those were exciting years for a young girl growing up. I look back on it now, and with my wisdom of the years I can see that other parts of the world were downtrodden, heartbroken, and filled with sorrow. But in my youth I wasn't concerned about them. I wanted to have a full life, filled with fun and laughter, which I did.

Recently late one night I was thinking deeply about my personal history and of what I should write. I know that many people of our family will read this, and to have a clear picture of the kind of person I am, they need to know some of my thoughts and desires and what sort of things that made me what I am today. Well, I suppose we all have skeletons in our closets. Things about ourselves that we shield from the world. To just break right down and confess them is a hard thing to do. But in order for you to know some things you must know, and I must enlighten you. From the time I was nine years old, I had a speech defect. I stammer. Even now at age 56 I find that so difficult to write. It caused me years and years of torture, of humiliation, of shame, of embarrassment, and so because of it I lived a good part of my life in seclusion. By that I mean I never gave readings in school if I could help it, nor oral composition, etc. I never spoke in a group if I didn't have to. That way I could hide from everyone my impediment. Nevertheless, I shed barrels and barrels of tears over my humiliation. People can be so cruel and uncaring. Even now, years later when it has almost left me, I cry inside and my heart breaks for anyone with this same speech defect. My heart truly goes out to them. Now I understand the real meaning of empathy. This was always a thorn in my side, but now so many, many years later I see wisdom in this weakness of mine, for it truly brings me closer to my father in heaven, for when I'm called upon to perform in public such as a talk or prayer, I rely almost solely upon him to help me. And can you imagine my joy when he does help me and I get through it without one time hesitating. He is so right when he tells us that we will become strong because of our weakness. So true.

I suppose I'm coming close to the time that I met my husband, Harold Wayne Williams. It was during the second world war in 1945. One of my old convent friends, Barbara Graham, lived in Edmonton, Alberta, and we corresponded frequently. She wrote asking me to spend the weekend with her. At the time she was dating a boy in the American army. When I got there, she and her friend had made arrangements for me to meet a friend, who turned out to be Harold. We went to the dance the Sat night at the NCO club. I wasn't very impressed with him. Altho he was very handsome in his uniform, I thought him to be very rude. Well, we didn't see each other again for

Rae at sixteen years old.

several months, and then he came down to Calgary to spend a few days. We got better acquainted, and he had a chance to meet my family.

In August I spent part of my vacation in Edmonton, and it was there that we fell in love and tentatively made plans to get married after he was discharged from the US air corps. Well, to make a long story short, he was discharged in the fall of that same year, and in Jan of 1946 he enrolled in school at Stillwater, Okla. We were married that summer, July 31st, and we were married in our home in Rideau Park. After spending a few days in the Canadian Rockies and at my home, we took the train to the USA. We spent a week with Harold's folks in Ardmore, Okla, then a week with his sister and her husband in Ada, Okla. From there we went to Stillwater and stayed there until Harold's graduation the next summer.

My life after I was married was a far cry from the life I had lived before I met Harold. We lived in very humble circumstances, and Harold was in school while I worked in a jewelry store. After his graduation, we moved our things to his folks' home while he looked for work. After finding employment in Okla. City, I remained in Ardmore until he could find a place for us to live. That was one of the loneliest (if not *the loneliest*) summers I have ever spent. I had nothing in common with his parents or their style of living or the place in which they lived. I was very unhappy and anxious to be with Harold again. Finally we found a house to share with an older woman and her son. She was divorced from her alcoholic husband at the time. Well, we lived there until after our son was born in January of 1948. To say my life there was almost a nightmare is to put it mildly. Her ex-husband kept coming around during the day while I was alone. He was always drunk and disorderly and would shout vile names in thru the window. Many, many times I called the police to come and take him away. It was all so horrible and frightening. I was thousands of miles from home, with absolutely no friends with the exception of one Mildred Norris who kept in touch with me. Harold decided we couldn't stay any longer. We moved our things to Ardmore and spent about a month with his parents. They were kind to take us in, and altho they themselves didn't have many luxuries and mostly just the bare necessities, at least they gave us a place to stay. Finally Harold found us a place to live in Okla. City, and we moved up there and for the first time in our married life began the task of living as a family.

We lived in Okla. City about three or four years with Harold working for the Diesel Power Co. Three years after our marriage, I made a trip home with Wayne, who was eighteen months old. We flew for the first

Rae and Harold before their marriage.

time, and it was a thrilling experience. I arrived home in July and spent the next four months with my family in Calgary. As I look back on it now, many, many years later, I see what a terrible mistake I made by being apart from Harold for such a long period of time. And my parents were equally wrong in encouraging me to stay. But being back among familiar surroundings in the life I knew so well was pure contentment for me. To be perfectly honest, I wanted to remain there and never return to Okla. I often wonder what Harold would have done had I written and given him an ultimatum that he would have to move to Calgary or give us up. Well, I'm happy that I wasn't that kind of person and that I let my conscience guide me into going back to live my life in the USA. That was my only trip home while my Dad was living. For it was only a matter of a few years later (four) that my Dad passed away.

I believe it was the following year that Harold went to work for Halliburton Services, and we were transferred to Great Bend, Kans. That was the beginning of many, many years with that company and of moving many, many times in the years to come. But they were happy years, and when Wayne was four Anne was born, then four years later in Texas Susan was born. We had three lovely children, and we were happy in our life making new friends and moving from place to place. I

Harold and Rae cutting their wedding cake, July 31, 1946.

suppose now looking back, the happiest years we spent were the seven years in New Mexico while our children were growing up. They were happy years having our children in school and becoming involved with them. Spending many weekends in the mountains camping, taking trips to Calgary to visit my Mother and sisters. We bought our first home in 1958 in Farmington, and we were happy and contented in making improvements each year as we could afford it. We loved our home, our friends, and Farmington. I wanted to remain there the rest of my life. I wanted everything to continue on and on without ever changing, but life doesn't stand still, and eventually it had to come to an end.

To say that we weren't religious during those years is a true statement as far as attending church regularly. But as I look back now, I can see that I was always looking for something concrete to hold on to. In Borger, Texas, we attended the Wesley Methodist church faithfully for over a year. We enjoyed it so very much, and it was a good feeling to have our children enrolled in Sunday school, and Harold was happy singing in the choir. In fact, one time he sang a solo and did very well. Those were happy years there. After we moved to New Mexico, we soon got out of the habit, and before long we were totally inactive where religious training was concerned. But always in the back of my mind was a deep affection and loyalty toward the Roman Catholic church. I suppose due to my years at the convent and of the things I learned there. Our doctor in Farmington was a Seventh Day Adventist, and a very fine man. One time I went to a seminar their church had on smoking. I was very impressed that they cared enough about other people to want to help them. Because of this concern, I learned a little about their belief. Of course, at the time I smoked, and altho the seminar was excellent, I didn't have a strong enough commitment to stop. It wasn't until a few years later that I really had the desire.

During the seven years in Farmington, we attended the Methodist church twice!!!! We were surrounded by *"fine"* upright Baptists, and they were constantly inviting us to church. But my impression of the Baptists wasn't the highest in the world, so of course we weren't impressed. One of our best friends, the Rogers family, lived just across the street and down the block a few houses. Rich was a Mormon, altho not active. Phyllis had taken the discussions years earlier but never went any further with it. One day while the two of us were out driving, she warned me about them and implied never to let them in my house or I'd never get rid of them. Strange that a remark such as that would change our lives completely in the years to follow.

As I look back upon my life, I see where my Father in heaven was always aware of me and watched me with great care and love. We took the discussions from the Mormon missionaries and learned much from them, altho at that time of our lives we weren't ready to accept the change that it would require. I suppose the only reason we consented to take the lessons was the fact that I had been so rude to them one day when they knocked on the door and woke me up from a nap. After closing the door on them so rudely, I felt very badly. Then later I met them at a neighbor's and had a chance to redeem myself. I felt that we became very good friends with Elder Dick Stephens. He was from Ogden, Utah, and for years after we corresponded at Christmastime. He was such a fine young man.

During this time I had written to Mother informing her that we were learning more about the Mormon church. She at once wrote informing us that should we continue and even consider joining the church, that she felt duty bound to remove my name from her will. My Father felt a great resentment toward all Mormons and had he lived would have resented this very much. Of course, all was safe as we didn't go further with it. At least not for a number of years.

Ironic as things are, it was just a little over a year later that Mother passed away. She fell at the front door of her home and in falling broke her hip. She lay on the floor completely helpless from Friday late afternoon until Sunday morning, when my sister Jo found her. She had surgery two days later to set her hip and four days later passed away. When I heard the news, I was overcome with grief. I could accept her death easier than the fact that when she desperately needed one of us, we weren't there to help. It took me many years to understand why she had to die in such a manner. Of course we went home to straighten out her affairs and settle the estate. To this day I miss my Mother, and she's in my thoughts so often.

I know that the veil between us and those who have passed on is very, very thin. That at times those whom we love can reach across and console us. While at home after Mother's death, twice I heard her footstep in the hall. Once when I was in her room sitting on her bed, I could hear her coming down the hall and putting her foot on the first stair. Again while I was in the basement going thru the trunk. Again she was walking in the hall and getting ready to come down to the basement. I felt as tho she were trying to come to comfort me. How grateful I am for that. Also when My Dad passed away, I couldn't be home for the funeral, but I had the most beautiful dream. Just our family was together, and we were all sitting in a beautiful park on the grass. Everything was green, and it was so peaceful. Then my Dad said it was time for him to leave, so we all arose to say goodbye. Next we looked into the setting sun, and there the rays from the sun were shining up over the mountain top, and we saw a bird flying in those rays, and soon he disappeared over the top of the mountain. I cried every time I tried to tell that dream. I think it consoled Mother, too, for she would ask me over and over to tell her about it. So you see my father in heaven has been close in the times when I needed him the most. How grateful I am. My dear parents, how they loved us, their children, and what a beautiful life they gave us. Who could have better parents? How marvelous to have the knowledge that we'll be together again never to be parted if we live the gospel principles while here on earth. There is no greater gift of knowledge that I could have.

Well, finally the day of reckoning came for me. One day in May or the early part of June, Harold came home to report that we had been transferred to Henderson, Ky. Well, of all the places in the world, that was the last place I wanted to live. I knew the climate was the complete opposite to New Mexico, and after years in Okla. I never wanted to return to that type of high humidity. But even though I promised him the heavens, nothing would dissuade him from moving there. We at once put our house up for sale, then waited for the right buyer to come along. But that day never came. The population of Farmington had dwindled considerably, and just on our street alone there were nine empty homes, and ours would make the tenth. Harold flew to Henderson to get acquainted with his job and left me at home with the children to take care of things. We had one buyer who was interested in the house but had no money. I held out till the very end, when I called a lawyer and asked what to do. He said to get out from under it and sign the house over to him. Well, this we did, and the man and his family just walked in and took over the most beautiful house on the street with all our many improvements, such as a fenced-in yard, lawn both front and back, patio with a beautiful $300.00 awning, and a brand new den which was an extension of our living room. We did all the improvements ourselves. My heart was broken, and nothing could console me. It was hard enough to leave Farmington with all our neighbors and friends, but to give our house away was too much. I could not be consoled. We spent the last two nights in Farmington at a hotel, so we left our little dog Hodge with our neighbors across the street. He was heartbroken and thought we had left him for good. So the morning we were to leave Farmington, we went by to pick him up. Well, you've never seen a happier little dog. He just had to show us his happiness and joy at being with us again. How he jumped from seat to seat barking and licking our faces and trying to let us know his joy. As if we couldn't tell. We all loved him so much we would never have considered leaving him behind, but he didn't know this yet. I'm sure years later he slowly came to know of the love we had for him. He was one of us and a real part of our family. This move was also so hard on Wayne especially. He was to graduate from high school the very next year. He didn't want to go either and leave all his friends behind. I'm certain it hurt him more than we ever realized. Anne and Susan were younger—and I don't believe it affected them as much. Well, we moved into our rented house in Henderson and left a few big items out on the carport for lack of room. We at once began looking for a place to buy.

About a week after we got settled in our rented house, Harold had had a slight accident at the breakfast table one Sunday morning. He lifted his cup and walked over to the stove to get another cup of coffee, when he dropped the cup on the floor. He bent over to pick it up and dropped it again. He came back and set down and started to talk, but his words were garbled and he couldn't speak plainly. We both knew immediately he had had a slight stroke. To say we were frightened was to put it mildly. The next week we found a doctor in Evansville, Indiana, just across the Ohio river. After examining him, he put him in the hospital and ran a number of tests. Nothing showed up concrete enough to call his seizure a stroke, so he was sent home. He recuperated and was soon back at work. Strangely enough, he's never had a recurrence.

It wasn't long before we all settled down to a normal life with the children in school and Harold back at work. We resumed our square dancing and got acquainted with two couples there in Henderson who took us around to visit the various clubs. From then on we went dancing every Saturday night at one club or another. In December we moved into our new house that we had just bought. As Christmas came closer and we heard from all our friends back west, the feeling of futility and loneliness engulfed me, and I felt as tho I could not go on. We had such a little bit of money and really not enough of the bare necessities could we manage. Not even enough to send cards to our friends. I was about to give up and let loneliness overtake me. So on December 23rd I just told my children that I was sick (I was) and went back to bed. It was in the morning and school was out, so the children could manage for themselves. As I lay in bed I prayed with all of my heart and soul for the Lord to let me die. I knew that I would surely lose my mind if I continued to live. I woke up every hour or two and could not believe how fast the time seemed to pass. Sometime during that day I had a dream. I was standing alone at the bend in a road and knew as I looked back at the long, straight road that that was my life as it had been, but now I was changing direction, and from now on my life would take on new meaning and I would travel in a different direction. In the early evening I knew I must get up out of bed. This I did, and as the next two days passed I had time to recall my dream. For a long time after (in fact years), I wasn't certain as to whether it was a dream or a vision, but now as I look back I'm sure it was a dream. Strange to say, the day before Christmas I was taken ill with an infection and confined to bed until it was cleared up. Those several days in bed gave me plenty of time to collect my thoughts and to be alone to where I could learn from my dream. Slowly, I realized that the Lord had surely answered my prayers. That he did let the "old " me die, and that he was giving me a new lease on life.

Needless to say, from that day on I was slowly becoming aware of the spirit within me, and I was being taught by the Holy Ghost. I truly was "born again". I could not quench my thirst for knowledge, and I would make weekly trips to the library to check out any and all books of a religious nature. These I would devour until the early morning hours. I would make notes and keep track of important items. Things that related to me.

Of course, too, at this time we became active church members again and began attending weekly the Bennett Memorial church there in Henderson, Ky. Bro Bill was the pastor and soon became my very good friend. He and I had many talks together, and of course he knew about my dream. He suggested I enroll in the Monday morning Prayer Group which met each Monday morning for an hour or two. It consisted of approximately fifteen women, most of them being old "seasoned" members of the church. I attended faithfully and for a long time enjoyed it so much. In the meantime, we attended Sunday school and church each Sun morning. But even that wasn't enough for me. I attended services Sunday night which I dearly loved, and prayer meeting Wed. nights. In the meantime I was studying and reading everything on religion I could get my hands on.

Well, slowly I was becoming dissatisfied with the prayer group. It seemed as tho we were not at one on our thoughts of what God was like. At least they were all of one opinion, but I felt out of it. I became so very discouraged and decided to drop out of it. I did and for a while kept on with my studies. By this time we had a new pastor, and slowly he and I became friends. We had many talks together, and he would help me analyze my dream. I knew it was a very special dream and that it had changed my life. I liked what I was becoming, and by noticing the change in myself I saw the good in others. He advised me to return to the prayer group, which I did. Well, I was happy to be back, but still that old uneasy feeling came back, and I was again very unhappy and dissatisfied. Ironically, at this same time the Mormon missionaries were coming by to visit, and altho I wasn't too interested in what they had to say, I was listening to them. Finally I had to leave the prayer group for good. It saddened me because I loved those women and wanted them to feel as I did. I was sure there was something wrong with me as I was so new in the church and these people were well seasoned "religious" women. And because of this I again felt very discouraged.

Well, the missionaries kept dropping by every few days, but nothing clicked. I just told them I was happy where I was and also if the Lord wanted me to make a change he would "*open*" the right door. Then it happened. One day Elder Bill Schwab from Central Pointe, Oregon, came by with his companion. He was such a happy, enthusiastic person and so happy with the knowledge he had. The first day he stayed about three hours. I never wanted him to leave. We talked and talked, and he just seemed to know exactly how I felt. I wanted his enthusiasm and happiness. I didn't know then how he got it, but I was determined to get it for myself. Now I know it was a testimony of the gospel, but at that time I didn't know. Slowly he and Elder Wayne Farnsworth taught me about the church. I showed them all my literature I had collected, and they were very impressed. Finally, the most important day of my life I suppose, they brought me the book "Jesus the Christ". From then on I was glued to its pages. As each page was read, I realized the truth of it and felt closer to Him than I ever had. Slowly, ever so slowly, I was being led to his true church here on earth. The Church of Jesus Christ of Latter-day Saints. As the missionaries came, we would talk for hours about the book and of how I felt, etc. Finally one day Elder Schwab said, "When are you going to be baptized? Our church is based on these teachings from this book." It seemed as tho a light came on, and I knew this was where the Lord wanted me. From that day on I began making preparations to leave the Methodist church forever and to become a Mormon.

THE CHURCH OF JESUS CHRIST OF LATTER-DAY SAINTS

Certificate of Baptism and Confirmation

Date March 16   19 67

Branch   MISSION

Henderson   ~~W&Y~~ E. Central States   ~~XXXXX~~

This Certifies that   Allie Rae Setterington Williams

daughter   of Harold Aubrey Setterington and   Mabel Alice Rogers
Son or Daughter   Father's Name   Mother's Maiden Name

Born Mar. 25, 1921 , at Calgary   , Alberta   Canada
Date   City or Town   County   State or Nation

was baptized March 16, 1967, by William Schwab   ,   Elder   , and
Date   Priesthood

confirmed a member of The Church of Jesus Christ of Latter-day Saints, March 16, 1967
Date

by   William Schwab   ,   Elder   .
Priesthood

Signed _Berry E. Tapp_   Signed _Frank R. Fults, Jr._
Clerk   Bishop—Branch President

PHOTO GALLERY

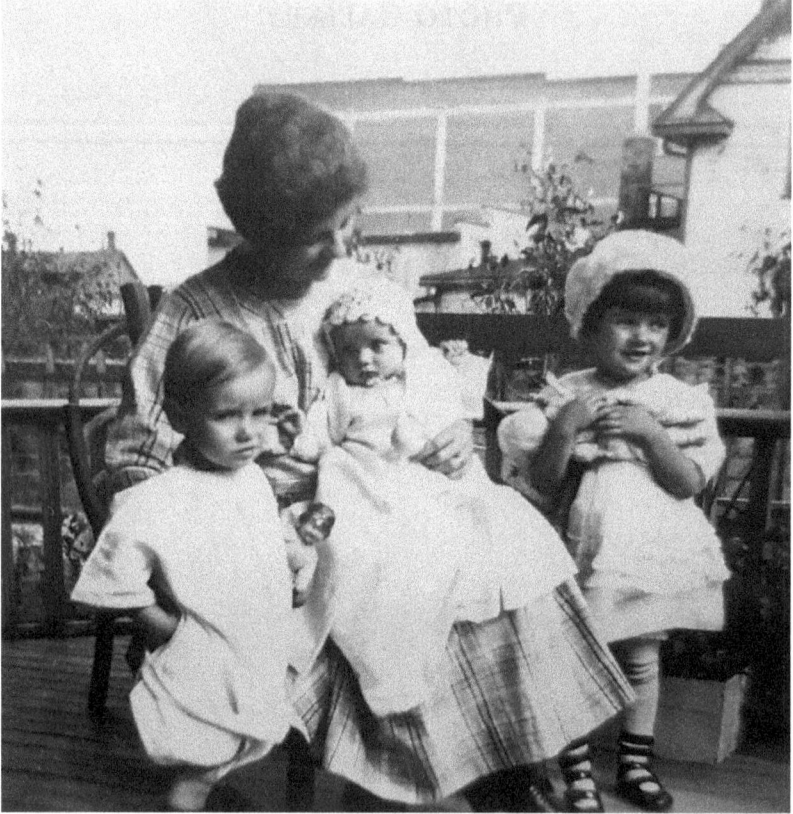

Aunt Allie with Jack, Rae, and Ruth.

Harold, Jack, Ruth, and Sylvester Setterington (Harold's father) holding Rae.

Jo and Rae.

Rae, Jo, Ruth, and Jack.

Rae, Mable, and Jack.

Ruth, Rae, and Jack.

Friend and Rae at the convent.

Rae at the convent grotto.

Bathing beauty Rae at home in Calgary.

Rae on the side of her home in Calgary. Note the beret.

New hairstyle!

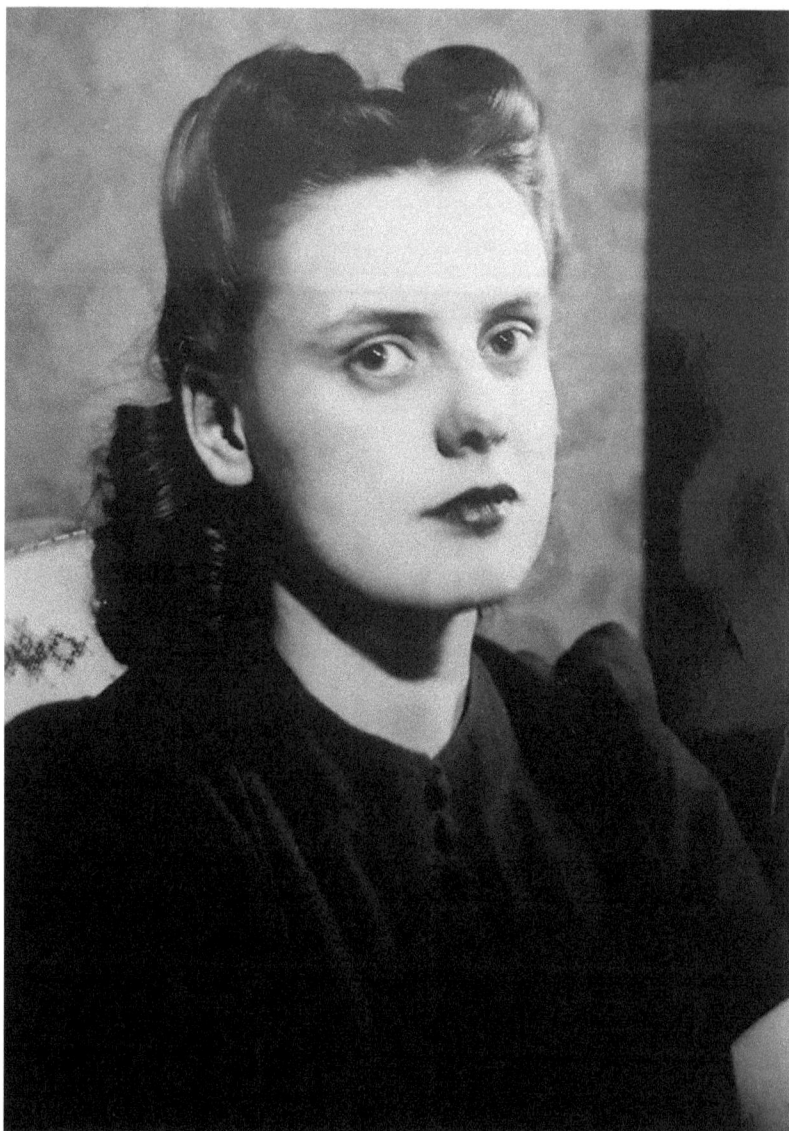

Rae with her great Aunt Allie.

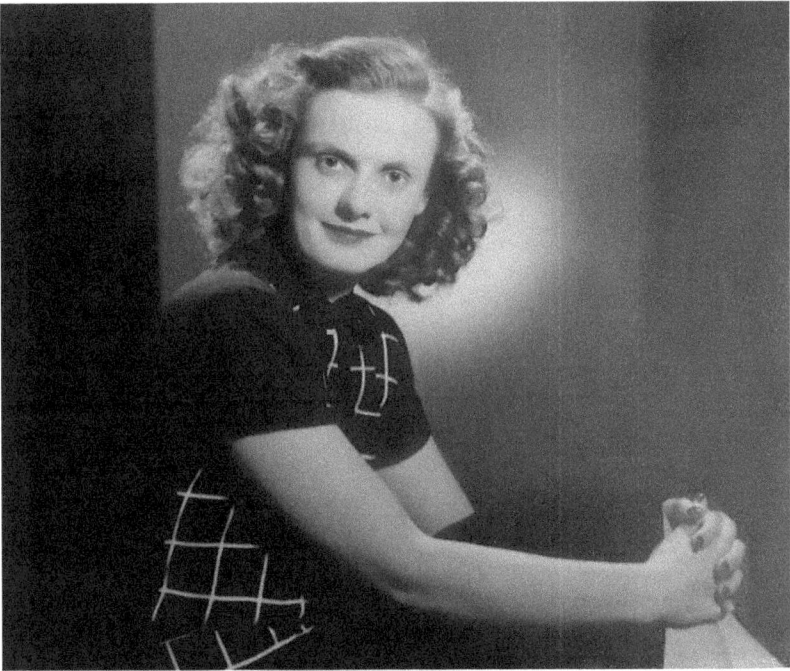

Glamour shot.

Harold and Rae, a short time after they were married.

Bow Valley at Banff.

Bow Falls at Banff.

Rae and Mabel.

Rae and Mabel.

Rae on June 14, 1996.

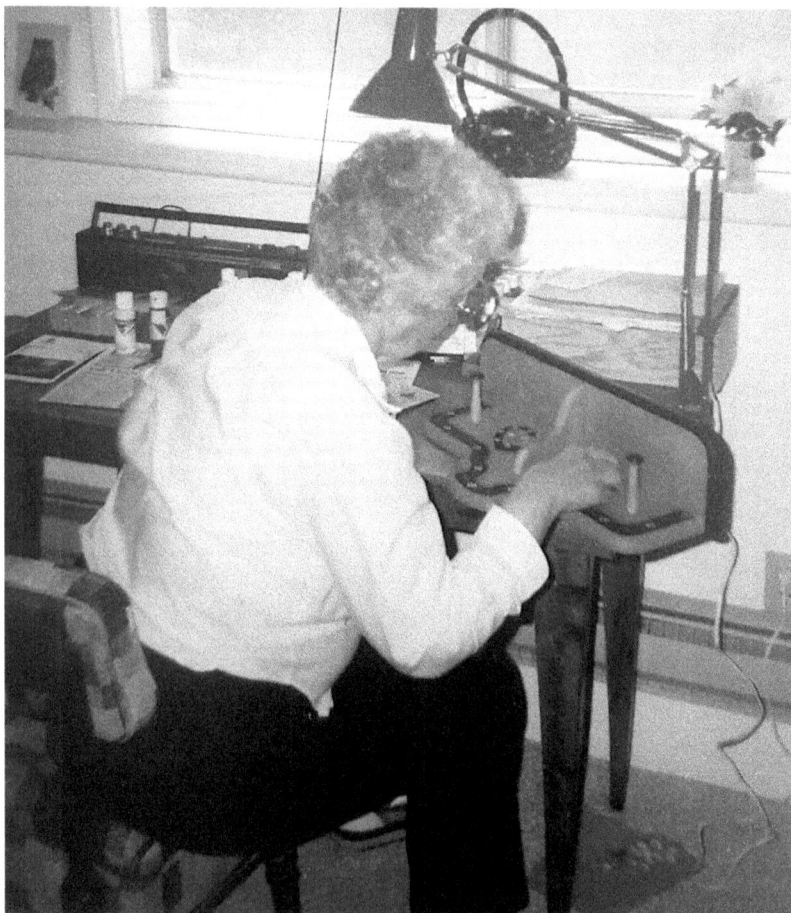

Tole painting.

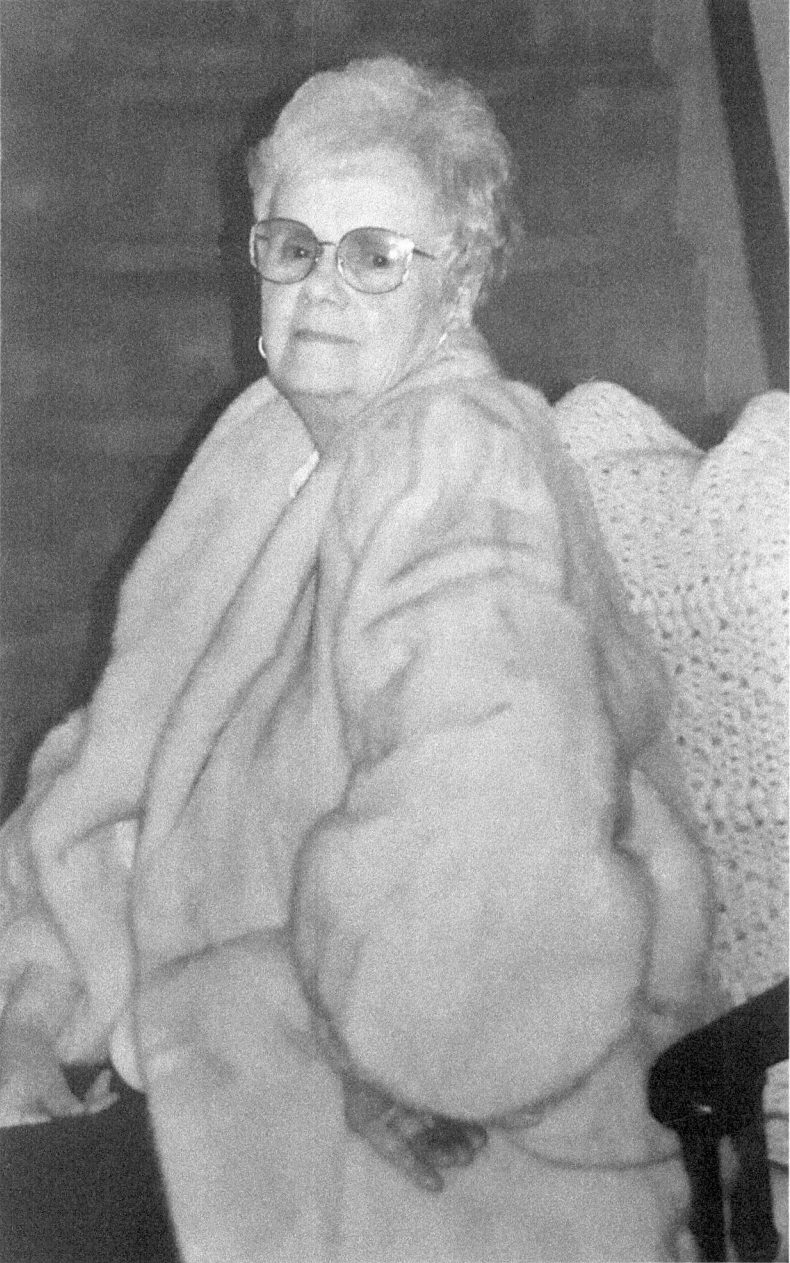

Glamour shot.

Jo and Rae in Rigby backyard.

Rae and Gerrie dancing in the Rigby living room.

Rae, Wayne, and Megan at Rigby.

BIOGRAPHY OF ALLIE RAE SETTERINGTON WILLIAMS, BY ANNE LYON, DAUGHTER

Allie Rae Setterington was born on a dark, cold, stormy morning on March 25, 1921, in Calgary, Alberta, Canada. Her mother told her later, when she was a little girl, that being born on that stormy day was where she got her sunny disposition. She was the middle child in a family of four girls and one boy. Ruth was her older sister, and Jack was her older and only brother. Jo and Gerrie were her younger sisters and the ones that she was always closest to.

Her mother was Mabel Alice Rogers Setterington, and her father was Harold Aubrey Setterington. Her parents were older when they got married. Her mother was 30 and her father was 35. They had five children relatively close together, which was hard on her mother's health. After Jo was born, Mabel was bedridden for quite a while, and maybe that was when her husband hired a live-in maid. From that time onward they had a maid, although it wasn't the same one for the whole time. There was a room off the kitchen which was for the maid.

I can remember one of the maids who was German. I was only about six years old, so I don't remember very much. I remember her polishing my white shoes with a bottle of white polish that had the applicator on the end, and she even polished the soles of the shoes.

The first part of this biography is taken from my memories of the stories that Mom would tell me as I was growing up. My brother, sister, and I would ask her to tell us stories of when she was young, and she was always happy to sit down with us together, or individually, and tell us story after story. I always thought she had the most wondrous childhood and home life. She was the best storyteller, and you could

Rae in December 1922, aged one year and nine months.

Harold Aubrey Setterington and Mabel Alice Rogers Setterington.

just imagine yourself being there with her as a child as she told the stories of growing up in a large family.

Every summer Mom and her family would pack up the car and go to Banff, where they rented a summer home on the lake. I think they stayed as long as a month. Their father had to work during the week, but he would join them every weekend. Mom would tell about when they first arrived at the lake and how all five children would help carry all the things in from the car, then change into their swimming suits, grab towels, and run down to the lake. She often thought how happy her mother was to have all five of her children occupied down at the lake and out of her hair

Mom's father was from Leamington, Ontario, and her mother was from Detroit, Michigan, and a couple of times he took the older three children, Ruth, Jack, and Rae, on a road trip back to those places. He'd go with a good friend of his, Ned Swanson. Jo and Gerrie would be left behind with their mother. This was such a fun time for everyone. They would be gone for quite some time, but their father would write home regularly to his wife and two little girls back in Calgary.

I remember Mom also telling about one time when her father went on a trip and she wasn't included, but it was during the cold months of the

Rock house at Banff.

year, because she remembered her mother turning up the thermostat on the furnace while he was gone and how nice it was to have the house nice and warm. When he was home, he insisted the thermostat be turned way down, and the house was pretty cold.

They all had dinner together every evening and sat in the dining room. Her mother had a bell that sat by her place at the table, and she would ring it to call the maid. Mom always felt bad for the maid. They all had their own sterling silver napkin rings with their initials on them. They would have linen "serviettes," not napkins. Napkins were a baby's diaper. As an adult, Mom never told anyone about having a maid growing up.

During the summer, the children in the neighborhood would walk over to the Elbow River, which wasn't too far from their house, and spend hours in the water having such fun. In the winter they would go ice skating on the same river. Mom's ankles weren't very strong, so she would skate around on the ice on the inside of her feet.

They would walk to school, even when the weather got to be below zero and the snow was so deep. The girls always wore dresses with heavy, knitted leggings underneath that would go up past their knees. In the spring, when it started getting warmer, the girls would roll the leggings down, and it would look like they all had donuts around their ankles.

At Christmas, her mother spent hours in the kitchen for days on end preparing Christmas goodies. One of the first things she would make during the season was fruitcake, because it needed to age for a few weeks before they cut it. After it was baked, she would wrap it in cheesecloth that had been soaked in brandy, then wrap it tightly in paper, tie it with string, and put it in the pantry to sit for a few weeks. After that, she would take it out and cover it with white marzipan and decorate it with red and green candied cherries, other colorful candied fruits, and pecan halves. She made tins of different fudges and candies that looked like they had come from a candy shop, they were so perfectly done and decorated. One of the things she made, that Mom passed down to her children, grandchildren, and great-grandchildren, was shortbread. There's a family secret that started with Mom that goes along with the recipe that we have all been sworn to never reveal. Another recipe that we all love but have a hard time making is peanut butter fudge, or PBF as we all call it now. It's divine!

Because Mom's mother spent so much time baking and making Christmas goodies and shopping for presents for everyone, she never had time to wrap the gifts. As the children got old enough to go out on dates, or just hang out with their friends, they would leave her home alone on Christmas Eve to finish preparations for Christmas morning. Everyone except Mom. She would stay at home and wrap up all the presents for her mother while her brother and three sisters were out with their friends. Christmas morning was always so fun, and their mother would have the biggest pile of gifts around her, and they all waited anxiously as she opened them all.

Later on in the afternoon on Christmas day, friends would come around to visit, and Mom's dad always had bottles of "adult beverages" ready to offer them all drinks.

They would put up their Christmas tree on Christmas Eve and decorate it. Then those that had plans with friends would leave for the evening. They left the tree up until late into January.

When Mom was about 8–10 years old, the doctor told her mother that she needed to have all the girls' tonsils out. He said it was to keep them all from getting sick so often and passing it on to each other. The night before the "big day," they were all given a bath and had their hair washed. Then they were put into clean pajamas and nightgowns. The next morning they all went down to the hospital and sat on the front steps while each one of them was called in. They had to decide who was going to be the first, and it was decided since Ruth was the oldest that she'd be the first. Jo was the last because she was the most scared. After a while they watched through the front door as one of the nurses walked across the hall carrying Ruth to her room after her surgery. Mom thought she looked like she was dead, with her head hanging back over the nurse's arm and her long hair cascading down. When it was Mom's turn, she remembered walking into the operating room and thinking it must look just like hell looked like.

Another time, when all the kids were young, the doctor paid them all a visit at home to give them their smallpox vaccinations. One by one he lifted them up to the kitchen table and gave them their vaccination on their upper thigh. He poked them several times in a circle shape with a needle and put the vaccine on to be absorbed through the tiny holes. After a few days the spot blistered up and then eventually scabbed over. After a couple of weeks the scab fell off, and they were all left with a scar on their thighs. I remember Mom's being pretty big—about an inch across.

At some point while all the children were still at home, they got a dog. He was a purebred black and white collie. They named him Tux because it looked like he was wearing a tuxedo. There was one of the rooms he wasn't allowed in. I'm thinking it was in their father's den, but I'm not sure. Anyway, Tux would lay on the floor in the doorway into the den with his head on his paws. After a few minutes he'd inch forward just a couple of inches until his paws were just through the doorway. Mom's dad would say, "Tux," and he would hurry and scoot back to where he was. This would go on several times. I don't know if he finally got his way or not. In the evenings, Mom's dad would go for a walk and take Tux. They'd walk up the street, and Tux would hurry ahead, but when he got to the street crossings, he'd turn around and wait for his "dad," and then they'd cross together.

Since we're on the topic of pets, we'll talk about Mom's fear of cats. She was scared to death of them. She said it was from the time when she was playing outside with her friends and they were playing hide and seek. It was her turn to shut her eyes and count. She leaned her head on her arms up against a big tree and began to count. When she

Rae with Tux as a puppy in front of the summer house at home.

was almost done, she heard this weird noise behind her, and when she turned around, there on the ground behind her was a mother cat having her kittens. Mom was completely freaked out, and from that day on she had a deathly fear of cats. She wouldn't go anywhere that had cats—clear up into her adult years. I remember having to go with her when she sold Avon so I could keep any cats away from her.

There were times Mom and her mother would go shopping and while they were out and about they liked to stop in at the fortune teller's shop and have their fortunes told. She'd serve them a cup of tea and when they were done drinking she'd read the tea leaves that were left by putting the saucer on top of the cup and flipping it over so the leaves fell onto the saucer. Something about how they were arranged on the saucer told her all she needed to know about them. It was from these experiences that Mom learned to "tell our fortunes" as children and grandchildren. It was so much fun and she was so good at it! She didn't tip the contents of the cup onto the saucer. She just read them straight from the bottom of the cup. If she didn't like what she saw she'd just smack the side of the cup a couple of times to rearrange the tea leaves.

She really played the part to the max. We loved it and had lots of good laughs. She could also read our fortunes by the creases in our hands.

When Mom was about 10–12 she and her girl friends started a sewing club. Every Friday night they'd all gather at one of their houses with their sewing kits and sit around and work on their embroidery.

It was around this time in her life, maybe a little younger, that she was out playing with her friend in the park. A man walked up to them and asked them if they wanted some candy. Her friend said no but Mom said yes and went with him to his apartment while her friend went home. Not needing to go into any details, Mom was abused. She ran home afterwards but never told anyone. She knew if she told her mother she'd be in so much trouble, so she just kept it to herself. Years later as an adult she told her brother and sisters, but they didn't believe her. When they were all married and most of their own children were grown and on their own, the five of them were all together and Mom brought up the subject of being abused when she was a little girl. Her brother, Jack, said, "Oh, are you still telling that same old story?" Jo and Gerrie eventually believed her as they got older. How hard it was for Mom to carry that burden and not have love and support from her very own family.

As she got older and into her teen years, her mother taught her how to bake. First she would have to wash her hands and clean her fingernails. Her mother taught her how to stir the cake batter with her hand, so it's a good thing she washed them first! It got to a be regular thing for her to stay home on Friday nights and make her dad his favorite cake—fresh orange layer cake with fresh orange sections on top. She'd also bake him bread.

Stories of Mom and her family members

Here are some stories about Mom and her family.

Her mother

Let's start with a few stories about Mom's mother, Mabel. Her children called her Mother. Mom loved her with all her heart and soul and tried her whole life to be helpful in any way she could. Mabel had a bit of a sad upbringing. At some point in her life at home her dad became an invalid. I got the feeling from what Mom said that he just kind of decided he was an invalid. I think he had asthma or something like that. He was mean to his wife and three children, Harold, Mabel, and Maude. He was emotionally and verbally abusive to all of them and was physically abusive to his son, Harold. All the children had to work from young ages to help with the family expenses. I know that Mabel and Maude were married at older ages, around 30 or so. I think this home life helped make my grandmother who she was. For some reason she was very class conscious and somewhat racist.

When her children were still pretty young she and her husband decided to buy a new house. They found one they liked, but while sitting out in the car after touring one of the houses, Mabel noticed that the neighbors next door were foreigners. Maybe Jewish, maybe German, I can't remember. But when she saw that she would be living next door to them that house was scratched off the list. She wasn't living next door to the likes of them!

One of my favorite stories that Mom would tell us was about the time her mother had all her lady friends over, dressed in their pretty dresses, hats and gloves for afternoon tea. They were all sitting in the living room holding the beautiful hand-painted china cups filled with tea from the silver tea service when Mom walked in after school. As they all looked up she blurted out, "Mother, what does f**k mean?" Cups and saucers and silver teaspoons rattled as all the women gasped in horror. I don't remember what happened to Mom, but I'm sure she didn't get to stay around long. Her mother was very prim and proper. Mom said she wouldn't say the word "breast" even if it was on a chicken. When a woman was pregnant she was referred to as "being sick." It was too indelicate to actually say the word *pregnant*.

Talking about "being sick," when Mom was old enough to have her first period (I don't know what her mother referred to that as) her mother took her upstairs and got her all fixed up with a sanitary napkin. As they were coming down the stairs Mom was walking awkwardly with her legs far apart. Her mother looked at her and said, "Rae, if you walk like that everyone will know what's going on." I can just picture her.

Mom "stammered" (she hated the word "stutter") up until she was a grown woman with children. This embarrassed her mother, especially when Mom got in her teen years. She sent Mom to elocution classes to help cure her of it, but they didn't work. One time Mom got an invitation to some lady's house for some occasion, and her mother wanted Mom

Family members in front of the summer house in Calgary. Sitting on the ground: Ruth's two sons, Tux the dog. Middle row: Mabel, Rae, Wayne, Mildred (Jack's wife), Harold, Ruth, baby Shannon. Top row: Jo, Jack, Gerrie, Bob (Gerrie's husband).

to call the lady up and tell her she would accept her invitation. Mom didn't want to because she would stammer, but her mother made her do it anyway. She stood by while Mom made the call, and listening to her stammer, she just snatched the phone away from her and finished the call herself. Because Mom was afraid to make the call in the first place, and was made to do it anyway, it made her stammer all the worse, and then to have her mother yank the phone away from her and complete the call made her feel just horrible.

This next story could just be in a section on its own, but it also tells a little about what my grandmother was like. It was when Mom was about sixteen that her parents decided they were going to send her to school up in Red Deer at Saint Joseph's Catholic convent. She was struggling in public school, especially with math, and they had heard there was a good all girls school program there. It was a couple of hours away by train and she would be living there and coming home every month or two.

To hear her describe it, it's just like what you'd picture in your mind of an old Catholic convent in the 1930s, a big, old, dark rectangular building of dark red bricks with lots of windows and stairs leading up to the front door. Lots of nuns in their black and white habits with their rosaries hanging from their belts. Lots of girls of all ages dressed in the same plain uniforms. In the winter mornings they'd be woken by a nun, and they'd stumble in the dark on the cold floor over to the wash bowl and pitcher and break the thin layer of ice off the top of the water so they could wash their hands and face and get ready for breakfast. Breakfast was cold, congealed, gray porridge. I think they had mass every morning and then went to classes. Very stern nuns taught the classes. Mom was left handed, and while the girls were working at their desks, the nuns would walk up and down the aisles keeping an eye on them. When they came to Mom, or any other girls writing with their left hand, they'd rap hard on their knuckles with a wooden ruler. It's probably one of the reasons she stammered. That and because she was sexually abused earlier in her life.

While she was living there, her mother would often send her goodie boxes in the mail. One of the things she always included was peanut butter fudge. All her friends were so excited when Mom got her boxes from home and would gather around in hopes of getting a little something. She would always share with them.

St. Joseph's Catholic Convent.

Mom loved it at the convent and made a few lifelong friends, two of whom were Sister Denise and Sister Anne, who were nuns and teachers there. I was named after them. Sister Denise's name before she became a nun was Cecilia, and then Sister Anne. Thus Cecilia Anne. Mom kept in touch with them through letters and cards and went back a time or two to visit after she was married and her children were grown. Each nun had a feast day, and Mom always sent a card and letter to Sister Denise on hers up until she died.

When Mom was eighteen, and still at the convent, she got really sick and had to go home to be treated. It was found out that she had appendicitis and ended up having to have her appendix removed. She was in the hospital for several days, and while she was there her mother spoke to the doctor privately and convinced him to tell Mom that she was too sick to go back to the convent. Her mother didn't want her going back because she knew that Mom really wanted to become a nun, and she sure didn't want that to happen. Mom was heartbroken when the doctor broke the news to her. I don't know how she ever found out her mother did that behind her back.

Rae with Sister Denise.

Her father, Daddy

Now a couple of things about her dad, Harold. She idolized him, yet was sort of scared of him. I think this was pretty commonplace in those days. The dad ruled the roost. He was very strict but was crazy about all his children. When it was their birthdays he would take each of them out to eat. Mom would tell us how she'd look forward to when it was her turn—how she'd rush home after school and have a bath and get dressed in her prettiest dress and put on her dress shoes and then hurry downtown to her father's office. The two of them would walk down the street together to a fine restaurant where they had finger bowls and little towels and have such a nice dinner and time together. Then they'd walk back home hand in hand.

Her father was an estates manager and had a big safe with his clients' valuables inside. Sometimes she would get to his office early on her birthday, and he would open the safe and show her some of the beautiful jewelry. Because of the job he had as an estates manager neither he nor his family were affected by the depression. Life just went on as usual for them, and they just lived their happy lives.

During World War II a lot of servicemen were stationed in Calgary and would be around for good times on the weekends. The young women who lived there were never short of dates and fun times. One winter night Mom had a date with a serviceman who came to pick her up at her home. Her dad was always very sure to meet the young men his daughters were going to go out with, so he was there when this guy came to pick up Mom. He visited with him for a few minutes, told him to have her home by a certain time, and sent them on their way. They went to a dance, and when it came close to the time Mom was supposed to be home, she told her date. He said he wasn't ready to go home, and if she was she could just leave. So she did. She didn't have any money for the bus or a taxi and ended up walking a long way home in the cold. When she was finally walking down the street her house was on, she could see the porch light shining out in front and her dad in his robe standing out on the porch. She didn't get into trouble, but her dad told her to never go out again without money in her purse, and if she didn't have money to come and ask him. It wasn't too long after that the police showed up at their house one afternoon and asked for her dad. They asked him if he owned a gun, and he said he did. When he went to get it, it wasn't there. The police showed him a gun they took from a

Ruth, Rae, Jack, and Harold.

young man who had gotten in trouble with the law. It was that same guy that Mom had had a date with earlier. They were able to trace the gun back to her father from the serial numbers on it. They never knew how he was able to get the gun. It had been in her father's den, so it probably wasn't too hard to take it from there.

Later in his life her Dad became diabetic. Her mother would can special jars of fruit just for him using saccharin.

After Mom had married, moved away from home, and had my brother, Wayne, she got a telegraph from her mother saying that her father had passed away. He had gone down in the basement for something and fallen. Jo, who was still unmarried and living at home, found him down there. He couldn't talk and just slurred his words and sort of drooled. Jo put her soft slippers under his head and stayed with him until an ambulance could arrive. While he was in the hospital, it was discovered that he'd had a mild stroke. Even though it was mild, he died shortly after. Everyone thought that when he heard that he'd had a stroke that he just gave up the will to live. His best friend, Mr. Swanson, who traveled with him and his children back to Ontario, had also suffered a stroke a while earlier, but his was very severe, and he ended up lying in bed for a long time fully incapacitated. Mom's dad was afraid of ending up like him. Mom wasn't able to go home for her dad's funeral because she couldn't leave Wayne, who was so small and sick with the measles. She always felt awful about that.

Ruth, her older sister

In their teenage years, Ruth and Rae didn't get along, and as they got older there was no love lost between the two of them. Ruth was jealous of my mother. I think it probably started when Mom was first born, but I don't really know. I do know that as she got into her teen years Ruth was very pretty, and so was my mother. When Mom got to be dating age, some of the boys that were interested in Ruth started being interested in Mom. That didn't go over well. Ruth went out of her way to be mean and hateful to Mom, and it carried with Mom all her life.

Ruth married Stuart King and had five children. I don't know what he did for a living, but they moved around a lot with his work, and they were quite well to do. They ended up settling in Calgary and had a gorgeous house within just walking distance from my grandmother's. I can remember walking over to her house from Maemo's (what we

Mabel and Harold. Mabel wrote on the back of this picture, "No, I haven't had a stroke. I was just smiling. Look at that darned man—not a day older in fourteen years—while I look like the Wreck of the Hesperus at the remains of a misspent life—and feel like it, too."

Ruth, Rae, Mabel, ?, ?, Mildred (Jack's wife), Gerrie, Aunt Maude, Jo.

called my grandmother, short for Mabel) through a pretty wooded area and over a suspension bridge, and right after getting off the bridge her house was just across the street. I can remember dancing in her living room to Cancan music and playing with her kids and going swimming with them at the public pool. When I was at this age I didn't know that she and my mother didn't get along, but there was just something about her that scared me. I don't know what it was—just her demeanor and crassness, maybe. Mom told the story about Ruth walking into a room in her house and finding the maid sitting on the couch. She told her to "haul her ass off that couch and get to work." Yeah, she wasn't a very nice person. No wonder she and Mom didn't get along. Mom was just the opposite of Ruth. Mom never let any of her friends know that her mother had a maid, and Ruth treated her own maids like dirt.

Jack: Mom's older and only brother

Mom didn't have too many stories to tell about Jack. She did say he was something of a stuffed shirt and couldn't take teasing, which Mom was always good at. His sisters called him "the professor" because he wore glasses and was so proper and sort of stodgy. He was pretty reserved and not a lot of fun. At some point he took up smoking a pipe, which added to his professorial look. I met him once when I was a teenager and thought the nickname fit him nicely.

One day Mom was in the kitchen mixing up a batch of bread and Jack came in. He started pestering her, and she finally picked up the big ball of bread dough she'd been kneading and threw it at him. He caught it and threw it back. He ran outside laughing into the backyard, and Mom chased after him with the dough. They ended up throwing it back and forth at each other and dropping it several times. By the time they were done goofing around, it was full of dirt, leaves, and grass.

It was probably around this time that Jack noticed that his friends that came over to spend time with him were now coming around to be with his sister Rae. That must've been an eye-opener.

Jo

When Jo was born, for some reason she needed to have a transfusion. Mom always remembered the scar on the inside of her arm from the needle. After she was born, their mother wasn't very well and ended up on complete bed rest for several months. As Jo got older, she wasn't much for looks and had a space between her two front teeth. She didn't have many dates and was sort of a tomboy. She loved horses, and if I remember correctly, her father bought her one. She was also a great speed skater and very athletic. She and Mom got along great. After Jo was married, she had two little boys in quick succession—less than a year apart. Her husband, Bob McKay, said he was going to stick his "manly parts" in the window and slam it as hard as he could, which maybe he did, because she never had any more children. Bob was an alcoholic and made Jo's life so very hard, but she never left him. She became a stewardess for some Canadian airline all their married life. Bob finally died of a lingering bout with throat cancer. Jo came to visit us several times through the years, and she was such a nice, gentle soul. I really liked her.

Gerrie: Mom's youngest sister

Gerrie was always the life of the party, and wherever she was, there was a laugh a minute. She was a handful for her mother to raise after her father died. I think she must've been still in her teen years. It was hard for her mother without her husband there to help. Gerrie had two pregnancies before being married and two abortions. That's all I know about that. I can only imagine how hard that was for her mother to cope with all on her own. No one's ever talked about that. My mother just mentioned it a couple of times to me.

Gerrie was finally married and had a baby boy by that marriage. Her first husband's name was Bob Allen. Their son's name was Randy. Gerrie never really treated him very nicely. She was divorced from his dad when Randy was a few years old, and she married a man called Alec Romalo, from Rumania. He was tall, thin, and swarthy and very nice and fun-loving. My dad called him Brother-IN-Law, accent on IN. Gerrie and Alec had two children, Roxanna and Sasha. Randy lived with them, but as I said, he wasn't treated very well. He was a little odd, but I thought he was nice the few times I was with him. Gerrie later divorced again after her kids were older and then married a childhood sweetheart, Smitty. His last name was Smith, and that's why he was called Smitty. I don't think I ever knew his given name. They had several happy years together, and then he died. Gerrie had him cremated, and as she said in her own words when asked what she did with his ashes, "I flushed them down the crapper." Nice. I liked Gerrie. She was always fun to be around.

Well, that pretty much covers all of Mom's immediate family. Even though there were some pretty raw things said about some of them, Mom loved her family and longed to be with them. Just as with any family, we all come away from them with lessons learned and things to overcome. Overall, Mom had an idyllic childhood and felt loved and secure. Most of us can't ask for more than that.

Boyfriends

Mom had lots of boyfriends as she got into her teen years and early twenties. The one she talked about most was Bruce McClellan. He was actually crazier about her than she was of him, but they dated for years and were great friends. Their mothers thought for sure they'd eventually get married. Bruce was actually my dad's best man when he and Mom were married. There's a sad little story to go along with that. Mom and Dad were married in her parents' living room, and after they left for their honeymoon, Bruce kept on drinking and drinking until he was pretty much sloshed, then followed them up to their hotel. They never saw him there, but someone told them he had been there. Years and years later, well over forty, Mom and Dad were visiting my aunts Jo and Gerrie in Calgary, and they heard that Bruce was dying of cancer. Mom went over to visit him and to say goodbye. Mom was sitting beside him, and he reached over and touched her beneath her eye. He said, "Oh, Rae, you still have those dark circles under your eyes." I always thought that was a tender time for two great friends that shared so many good times in their younger days.

Jobs

Mom's first job was as a dental assistant. In those days you didn't need to go to school to train to be a dental assistant. The dentist just hired you and then trained you on the job. Mom loved that job. She'd always wanted to be a nurse, so this was the next best thing. She mostly handed him instruments as he needed them, and then she'd make crowns and things like that. She did tell us about the time a man came in in excruciating pain with his jaw all swollen. He had an abscessed tooth, and the abscess had spread into the inside of his mouth and into his jaw. The dentist asked Mom to help hold him down and to watch out, because as soon as he lanced the abcess it would spew out all sorts of puss and blood all over the place. So she held the patient down and the dentist went to work. The man screamed out in pain, and puss and blood spewed out of his mouth all over the place. I guess it was Mom's job to clean up after that.

I don't know how many years Mom worked for the dentist or why she quit, but after that job she went to work for Henry Birks and Sons, which was a very fine jewelry store in Calgary. She worked in the fine china department at the back. She loved that job, too. She always looked forward to when they'd get new shipments in and was able to unpack the barrels and see what had arrived. I think she must've spent a lot of her paychecks in that department, because she had a lot of pretty what-nots and things that she'd bought from there. I remember them sitting around on doilies or on bookcases in all of our houses and having to be careful around them when we were dusting the furniture.

Mom had a few Royal Doulton figurines of old fashioned Victorian women in their pretty dresses and hats—all made in porcelain and hand painted—also lots of little porcelain animals, sheep, horses, ducks, geese. She had a couple of porcelain Coleport flower arrangements and a pair of Coleport earrings. I still have a Morecroft miniature vase that she bought from there. One of my granddaughters has a Royal Doulton figurine that was hers. I don't know what happened to most of those things, but I know that through the years a lot of them had gotten broken and glued back together.

It was during this time that Mom wanted to learn to smoke. It was the popular thing to do, and she wanted to fit in with the crowd. She said she would spend a lot of time behind closed doors up in her bedroom practicing smoking in front of the dresser mirror.

Harold and Rae

Before talking a little about Mom and Dad's wedding, I should tell something about how they met. Dad was stationed up in Edmonton, and they first met on a blind date. They must've hit it off pretty well, because there were more dates after that. Mom told us how all the women that worked for Birks Jewelry Store would just swoon when Harold would pass them walking to the back of the store where the fine china department was to pick her up after work or to go to lunch. I don't know how long he was stationed in that area, or how long they dated, but he eventually was discharged from the Air Force, and he went back to Ardmore, Oklahoma, where his parents were. He proposed before he left, and they wrote while they were apart. Then he came back in July, and they were married in her parents' living room on July 31, 1946.

Mom was dressed in a pretty pastel blue suit with matching hat and gloves. She was just beautiful. I don't remember her saying too much about their wedding, but there were many friends there, and her dad served Pink Lady cocktails. I can't remember where they went on their honeymoon, but I do know originally they had reservations at the Banff Springs Hotel. I believe they changed the date of their wedding at some point, and then they weren't able to get reservations there anymore.

After their honeymoon, they said goodbye to everyone and goodbye to Calgary and moved back to Dad's hometown of Ardmore, Oklahoma. Mom was never to live close to her home in Calgary again, but only able to take trips every couple of years for visits.

Harold, Rae, Jo, and Bruce.

Places they lived

Oklahoma

Moving to Oklahoma was a real eye-opener for Mom, to say the least. The weather was hot and muggy. Ardmore was a little farming community with farmers and their families suffering from the effects of the depression. She had come from a big city in Canada, and her dad provided a comfortable living for his family. They lived in a beautiful home and enjoyed many of the nicer things in life. One of the first things she noticed when arriving in Ardmore were so many jobless men sitting around on the streets talking and smoking. Mom and Dad's first house was mostly a little shack, from how she described it. There was a space under the door where you could see the light of day shining through and where the grass and weeds grew up through from outside. I don't know what Dad was thinking when he brought her there for the first time.

I think they might have moved to another place or two after that first place and eventually moved to Oklahoma City. I don't know if it was so

Harold Setterington, William Henry Williams (Harold's Father), Rae, Harold, Pearl Matt Vance Williams (Harold's mother).

that Dad could go to school or because of a job offer that they moved there. It was there that Mom became pregnant with Wayne. She was a couple of months along when her parents came to visit. She didn't dare tell them she was pregnant. They would've blown a cork. The first thing her dad did was go through the house and change all the light bulbs to higher wattages, and then he bought them some real butter. They all took a trip down to Ardmore to meet my dad's parents and spend some time with them. I've often wondered what the two sets of parents thought of each other. They were so completely opposite of each other. I do know that Mom's dad took her aside before they left to go home to Calgary and told her that if she ever decided she wanted to come home to just let him know, and he'd send her the money for the trip home. That pretty much says what he thought of the circumstances his daughter was living in. She never took him up on his offer and stayed with Dad through thick and thin, making each of their homes as nice as she could.

After Wayne was born on January 8, 1948, they moved to another house that they shared with some other people, one of whom was divorced from her alcoholic husband. When he drank he got mean,

Harold, Rae, and Harold in Oklahoma.

and one night he came to their house drunk. His wife locked him out. She, Mom, and her brand-new baby were there alone. He was raging mad and banged on the door and windows yelling and cursing at them and threatening them. He told Mom he was going to take her little baby away from her. That was it. When my dad got home, she told him what had happened, and they packed up and moved in with my grandparents, Mama Matt and Granddaddy, back down in Ardmore on Lake Murray Drive.

My dad would be gone all week long and then come to Ardmore on the weekends. That left my mother alone with the baby and with her in-laws. There was no love lost between Mom and my grandmother (Mama Matt), but she really loved my grandfather (Granddaddy.) I think Mama Matt thought Mom was too high and mighty. I was sort of afraid of Mama Matt myself. She looked grumpy and mad all the time. In one of their conversations she said to Mom, "Well, you knew where the boy lived when you married him."

So here was Mom living with her in-laws with a brand new baby, and to make matters worse he had horrible colic and cried all the time. Mom would be up all night long walking the floors with a screaming baby trying to sooth him and keep him from waking her mother- and father-in-law. She was exhausted all the time. One morning one of Mama Matt's friends came to visit. Mom had been up all night with her colicky baby and had just gotten him to sleep and crawled back in bed herself when the friend knocked on the door. She had came to see the new baby. Anyway, when Granddaddy asked Mama Matt if they ought to just let Mom sleep since she'd been up all night, she just said gruffly, "Get her up."

Another time Mom was holding her tiny baby when Granddaddy came over to her and lifted the nightgown and started to blow pipe smoke on the baby's stomach. He said it'd cure the colic. Mom snatched the night gown back down and told Granddaddy what for. These folks were from Eastern Kentucky and had some odd hillbilly ways that were totally alien to my mother from Calgary, Alberta, Canada.

Eventually Mom and Dad were able to move out of Mama Matt and Granddaddy's house and get a place of their own. Maybe it was back in Oklahoma City, but I'm not sure. Mom tells the story of one time when Dad had invited some friends to dinner, but there was absolutely nothing to make a nice dinner and no money to buy anything. So, Mom walked down to the little grocery store, pushing Wayne in a baby carriage, and asked if she could get credit to buy a few groceries. I don't recall how much her groceries cost, but it was only two or three dollars, and she was able to get everything she needed to make a delicious dinner of fried chicken, potatoes and gravy, a vegetable, and a homemade lemon pie for dessert.

Kansas and then Texas

Their next move took Mom and Dad to Kansas. I don't know if it was because Dad got a job with Halliburton at that time, but I'm sure it was for a new job. It was while they lived in Hays that I was born, on November 25, 1951. They lived in a couple of towns in Kansas and then after a few years were transferred to Borger, Texas.

Borger, Texas, was where their last child, a little girl, Susan Kay, was born, December 21, 1955. She was the apple of their eye. They'd sit for hours watching as she lay gooing and gahing on a blanket on the floor in front of them. They had finally been able to buy some nice new traditional furniture—forest-green couch and matching chair, floral brocade platform rocker and accent tables, and what-not shelves of solid mahogany. They had a record/radio console that opened up in the front and had pretty brass hardware. It was before we had a TV, and Wayne would sit in front of it and pretend he was watching TV. Mom had a laundry room right off the kitchen that had the back door in it. She had an old wringer washer and would do her laundry back there and then head out the back door to hang it on the clothes line. I can remember keeping horny toads in a shoebox back there in the laundry room. Mom made sure to always wear good sturdy shoes when she took the laundry out to hang in the backyard because there were hundreds of goat-head stickers back there, and she sure didn't want to get one of those in her foot! Our Aunt Jo came to visit while we lived in that house, and Mom always got a kick out of telling us about the time that Jo was helping with the laundry. She had just finished running a batch of laundry through the wringer and was getting ready to go out in the backyard to hang it on the clothes line to dry. She had on a pair of sandals, and Mom warned her that she'd better get on a pair of good shoes because of all the goat heads. Jo just waved her off and headed on out the door. A few seconds later she was screaming bloody murder and jumping up and down with goat heads in her feet.

Those things could go through a thin sandal sole and right into your foot. And boy did they hurt!

That was the first house we lived in in Texas. We moved to our next house, which didn't have any lawn. My dad told the landlord that he would plant the lawn for him, and so we ended up with a nice yard.

Mom was an excellent housekeeper. Our houses were always neat and tidy. One day one of her friends came over to visit and brought her black and tan dachshund named Sniffer. She and her friend were enjoying a cup of coffee and chatting away in the living room when Sniffer came out from behind the couch with an old dried-up biscuit. Mom was mortified. I'm sure they got a good laugh out of it, though.

Farmington, New Mexico

When Susan was nearly two years old , I was nearly seven, and Wayne was close to 11, Dad got transferred to Farmington, New Mexico. He went ahead and found us a place to live—the first home they'd ever owned, on 5003 Kayenta Drive. It was a flat-top, stucko house with reddish-pink wood trim. It was in the Highland View subdivision, where all the houses looked basically the same. Allied Van Lines packed us up in Borger, Texas, and moved us into our new home in Farmington. I remember Mom and Wayne sitting on the floor and leaning against the wall just opposite the front door. Mom was smoking a cigarette and wearing pedal pushers and watching the men move in our things. Susan said the first memory she has of that house was walking over to the big picture window in the living room and looking way up at the window sill. It was exciting times! We eventually got all settled in and began our lives on Kayenta Drive—some of the best years we'd had so far.

Mom and Dad worked hard to fix up our new home and yard. They spread grass seed front and back, and Mom would go out every hour or so to water it until it came up. In the backyard it was another story. Dad had put in posts for our fence, but he hadn't gotten the fence up. Our yard backed onto an open field, and the grasshoppers were fierce. They kept jumping from the field into our yard and eating off the new grass right to the ground. One day my dad decided he was going to hang some blankets up back there between the fenceposts. While he was stretching one across between the fenceposts, Mom called out and asked him if he was just going to stand out there from now on until the grasshoppers quit eating the grass. She thought that was hilarious—Dad not so much.

The two of them worked hard many hours on our yard, and it was one of the nicest in the neighborhood. They'd go out and dig the dandelions out of the grass, and Mom would spend nice times sitting on the ground out front by the little picket fence that separated our yard from the yard next door, cutting the grass that was too long between the slats of the fence while visiting with our neighbor Ann Small.

After living there a few years, Mom decided she'd like new furniture. She just loved the Early American look that was popular in the '60s. So we all piled in the car and drove down to Albuquerque to buy some furniture. Mom found everything she wanted and made arrangements to have it delivered. Meanwhile, she hired an interior decorator who advised her on new colors of paint for all the walls and made drapes for the kitchen and living room and also made matching ruffled chair pads for our ladder-back chairs. When it was all brought together it was so pretty, and Mom just loved it. She did get put out when our neighbor across the street, Gwen Adcock, came over with a friend of hers so she could show her through our house. Mom told her no, she didn't think she'd let them do that, and sent them on their way.

When Mom's mother passed away and she got her inheritance, one of the things she did was to have an awning put up over the patio that dad had built in the backyard. It was a wonderful place to sit or play in the summer. Mom liked to lay out in the sun in the summer and work on her tan. She had a brown halter top and a pair of shorts she'd wear. She'd have us kids rub baby oil on her back while she slathered the rest of her body, and if she got too hot we'd spray a fine mist of water on her with a spray bottle. She loved getting tanned, but my dad didn't like women with tans. That didn't stop her.

While they lived in Farmington, they began square dancing and had such good times. My dad became a square dance caller, and eventually they started their own club—The Roadrunners. They had a couple of hundred members by the time we had to move again. They had so many hours of fun and made so many wonderful friends. Mom was a great seamstress and made several square dance dresses for herself and matching shirts for dad. She'd spend hours sewing yards and yards of fabric, lace, and rickrack together into show-stopping outfits.

We took many vacations while living in Farmington. Each summer we'd take turns going to Calgary to visit Mom's family or to Ardmore to visit Dad's family. Those were fun trips.

Phyllis and Rich Rogers, with Rae in the middle, camping at La Plata Canyon.

One year we got a fold-out camper, and from then on every other week we'd go up La Plata Canyon to camp. Mostly we went with our friends Phyllis and Rich Rogers, who lived down the street from us. They had a fold-out camper too. We'd park by the river high up in the mountains and spend the whole weekend. It was great fun. At night we'd warm large rocks in the fire and then put them in the bottom of our beds so it'd be warm when we climbed in. One time Phyllis caught her bed on fire with one. I think after that we wrapped them in foil before tucking them under the covers.

It was also after we lived in Farmington that we had our first encounter with the Mormon missionaries. Mom and Dad's friend Rich Rogers was an inactive member of the LDS church, what they called a Jack Mormon. The missionaries would go over to their house now and then, and even their twin sons, Larry and Garry, were baptized when they were eight. (I remember the two of them running up and down the street yelling, "We've been saved! We've been saved!") Anyway, we had gone to church in Borger, Texas, a few times to the Methodist church, but we only went

Susan, Anne, Wayne, Rae, and Harold, all dressed up for Easter in 1960.

on Easter Sunday when we lived in Farmington. (Mom made Susan and me the most beautiful Easter dresses.) Eventually we didn't even go to church. Anyway, for some reason, Phyllis, Rich Rogers' wife, sent the missionaries over to our house one afternoon when they were visiting over at her house. Mom was having a nap at the time, and when she heard a knock on the door, she was not a happy camper being woken up from her nap. She went to the door, and after the missionaries introduced themselves, she said she was certainly not interested and slammed the door in their faces. She felt bad about doing that, so a few days later she had Phyllis send them back down. She and Dad took the discussions at that time but weren't baptized. I'm sure the fact that Mom's mother telling her she'd leave her nothing in her will if she joined that church might have had something to do with it.

Mom had always wanted to be a nurse, so when it came to taking care of her family when we got sick, she was the best caregiver. If we had a chest cold, she would rub our chests with Vicks or this awful pink, smelly stuff called Numotyzene. She'd smear it all over our chests and backs, then wrap a folded towel around us and pin it in place. She'd put Mentholatum under our noses and tuck us snuggly in bed. In the morning she'd wash the gunk off our chest with a warm, wet wash cloth and give us cream of wheat and toast cut into triangles or strips and sprinkled with cinnamon sugar.

Mom was always up in the mornings to help get us ready for school. Dad was never there because he had already left for work after Mom fed him breakfast and got his lunch packed. We'd have cold cereal, cream of wheat, or maybe a soft-boiled egg and toast. She'd show us how to crack around the top of the egg with the edge of our spoon and lift it off, then scoop the egg out onto a plate. She'd pack a sack lunch for each of us. The sandwiches were cut diagonally and wrapped in wax paper. The homemade cookies were stacked just so and also wrapped in wax paper. If we had an orange, she would cut a little off both ends and then cut shallow lines evenly spaced from top to bottom all around the orange so it was easy for us to peel when we ate our lunch. The top of the brown paper sack was folded down neatly, and she printed each of our names on each of our sacks and put them on the footstool along with two pennies for milk. When we got home in the afternoon after school, we always knew she would be home waiting for us, or down the street a house or two visiting with a neighbor. We always knew where to find her. She was always up to fix breakfast for us and always had a hot dinner waiting for us up until we left for college and got married. On cold, snowy, winter mornings we would come down the hall to find that she had set our boots by the furnace vent so they'd be warm when we put them on before leaving for school. She sewed all our dresses and probably some of Wayne's shirts. The girls didn't wear pants to school in those days, so we had to have lots of dresses to wear to school. When Mom did the laundry, she'd fold all our clothes so nicely and put them carefully away in our drawers. (It wasn't until after I had gotten married that I realized why the clothes in my drawers back home were always so neat and tidy.) Our house was always neat, clean, and tidy. She cleaned house and did laundry every week. In so many ways she truly made our home heaven on earth.

After living seven wonderful years in Farmington, Dad came home one day to announce that he had been transferred to Henderson, Kentucky. Mom was just sick. She loved her home and all her friends and couldn't imagine having to leave them. She told Dad that he would have to have an air conditioner put in our car before we left, and when we got there he'd need to buy some refrigerated air conditioners for the house. She wasn't going to live in the heat and humidity without refrigerated air.

Henderson, Kentucky

So on we moved across the country to Kentucky, arriving in the summer of hot, muggy weather. We rented a house the first few months after moving there until Mom and Dad could find a house to buy. Mom was pretty upset about the move and became sick and spent a good deal of time in bed. I didn't know it then, but now I know she was extremely depressed. Our first Christmas there I decided to make shortbread for the first time. I would beat the butter for a while, then take it into Mom, who was in bed, to look at. Then she'd tell me it needed to be beaten a while longer. I'd go out to the kitchen and beat it a little while longer, then take it back in for Mom to check. I did that a few times until I got it right, and then I finished making it.

Mom was looking for something missing in her life and decided that we ought to start going to church. We started going to Bennett Memorial Methodist Church. We loved it there. So many of my friends from school went there, and Mom and Dad made lots of new friends too. We'd go to morning Sunday services, then Mom and I would go again in the evening. I went because my friends were there. Mom went for more spiritual reasons. She also went to prayer meetings on Wednesday during the day. It brought a lot of comfort to her, and she became a happier person. She made lots of friends, and they all enjoyed being together to discuss teachings from the scriptures.

Mom and Dad started square dancing shortly after we moved to Henderson. I remember how thin my mother got after being sick for so long after we moved there, and how thin she looked in all her pretty square dance dresses. Square dancing was a good way to make new friends, and they had lots of good times.

Mom and Dad finally bought a new house for us at 1803 Old Madisonville Road. It was on a highway that wasn't too busy and out in the country. We were actually on the outside of a neighborhood, facing a field across the highway. It was here that Dad decided to start another square dance club. Our new house had an unfinished basement that two squares of dancers could fit into nicely. This new club became known as the Bluegrass Twirlers. It was at the beginning of this new club that a pair came—they were brother and sister-in-law. I don't remember

Harold and Rae, ready for square dancing. Rae made her dress.

the brother's name, but his sister-in-law was a friend of mine, Linda Coots. They were Mormons.

Because of the good relations Mom and Dad had with the missionaries in Farmington, they asked the Coots to send the missionaries to our house. It didn't take long for the Coots to act on that! Hardly anyone in the mission field ever got a request for the missionaries! Eventually Elder Schwab and Elder Farnsworth showed up at our door. They were an instant hit, and Elder Schwab and Mom became fast friends. He had answers to all her questions, and if he didn't, he helped her find them. She had finally found what she was looking for in the LDS church and after the whole family taking the discussions, Dad came to Wayne, Susan, and me one day and told us that Mom wanted to be baptized into the LDS church. He said we could all be baptized with her, but if we weren't ready then, he would wait with us until we were. Then the four of us would be baptized. We decided it was an important move for our family and that we ought to do it as a family. To say that we were all thrilled about the idea would be a lie. Wayne wasn't too thrilled, and I really wasn't because I felt like I'd be leaving all my friends in the Methodist church behind—until I realized I'd still see them all at school.

So we went to Church as a family that next Sunday. Henderson only had a small branch of the church and only had the first phase of their church building. We had church in the multipurpose room with folding chairs and a movable podium up front. I was totally unimpressed. We had just come from one of the cornerstone churches in Henderson with a beautiful, huge, red brick building that had white columns and a huge set of wide stairs leading up to the big front doors. There was even a balcony inside! Now here we were sitting on folding chairs? The missionaries were out in front to greet us, and everyone was thrilled to have a whole family of investigators come to church. Someone offered to take Mom's coat and hang it up for her, but she declined and clutched it tighter around her. There's definitely some symbolism there. Poor Mom.

After church we stopped off at our favorite restaurant for Sunday dinner. Little did we realize that was one of the last times we'd eat out on Sunday. After joining the LDS church, we no longer shopped or went out to eat, as this would cause other people to have to work, and Sunday was supposed to be a day of rest.

When we got home, square dancing friends of my folks, Voncile and Nolen Green and their daughter, Karen, came over. They came to try to talk Mom out of getting baptized and were there quite a while. It didn't help things for Mom to have them come over, since going to church had been hard enough for her. All in all, it had been one of her worst days.

We were baptized a few days later after Primary let out on March 16, 1967. That's back when Primary was held during the week after school. It seemed like every Primary kid was hanging over the side of the baptismal font. Mom was not too keen about having all of them there. One of the things my parents had to do to be worthy to be baptized was to quit smoking. It was part of the Word of Wisdom. Dad didn't have too much trouble quitting—his challenge was not drinking coffee. Mom had a really hard time quitting smoking, but she was a nonsmoker at the time of her baptism. Dad always joked that you could hear the sizzle as she put her last cigarette out just as she was being submerged in the waters of baptism.

Mom was so excited about joining the church that she went to all her friends in the Methodist church and told them about the LDS church and some of its teachings. She didn't want them to come back to her later in this life or the next life and accuse her of not telling them. Consequently most of them got mad at her and some of them never spoke to her again.

Now that we were all members of the Church of Jesus Christ of Latter-day Saints, we all made our adjustments and grew to love the people in our little branch and were given callings to help us grow and get stronger in the gospel. It was the best thing that had ever happened to our family.

Shortly after being baptized, we went to Hopkinsville, Kentucky, for what was called "mission conference." It was where all the wards and branches in the area met during the morning for two hours and then again for two hours in the afternoon after lunch. We listened to speakers and sang hymns. During the break between morning and afternoon session, the mission president came up to us as we sat out on the lawn eating our picnic lunch. He asked Mom and Dad if they would say a few words about their conversion to the Church in the afternoon session of conference. My dad said no, Mom said yes. You must remember she still had a bit of a stammer at this time, and she had never spoken in front of so many people ever before. This was a huge step for her to take. She did great. From that time forward her stammering gradually lessened until a few years later it was completely gone.

For a while after being baptized, Mom still had a problem giving up smoking. She tried so hard. She'd have one of us kids walk down the road to the little convenience store to buy her candy bars to help her keep from smoking. I don't know how many Oh Henrys she went through. She spent a lot of time in the unfinished basement during this time. When I'd call down asking her what she was doing, she'd just tell me she was closing the windows. At some point I was down there by myself and found a package of cigarettes and her lighter up in the rafters. Now I knew what she was really doing. The next time she went down there and I called down asking what she was doing, she said, "Just closing the widows so the rain won't get in." I called back "It's not even raining." The jig was up. Needless to say, she was finally able to kick the habit, but it was one of the hardest things she ever had to overcome.

Two years after joining the church, we took a road trip out to Salt Lake City to be sealed as a family for all eternity in the Salt Lake Temple. Mom and Dad invited the missionary that they first took the lessons from in Farmington, Dick Stevens, who lived in Ogden, Utah, and also Elder Schwab and Elder Farnsworth, who had baptized and confirmed us. Elder Schwab lived in Salt Lake, and Elder Farnsworth came all the way from Henderson, Nevada.

Wooster, Ohio

In the summer of 1967 or 1968, Dad came home to tell us that he had again been transferred, this time to Wooster, Ohio. I don't think this move was as hard on Mom as the one she had made to Henderson a few years earlier. The moving van came, packed us up, and moved us up to Ohio. We first lived in a rental house on Sherman Road.

While living here, Wayne joined the Air Force and left home. He was stationed down in Columbus, Ohio, where he met a girl named Susanne. They dated a while, and we went down there to meet her family when they became engaged. They were pretty much your typical Italian family. Wayne and Susanne were married in April, but I don't remember what year. They lived down in Columbus, and when Wayne got stationed somewhere else, Susanne went back to live with her family. Something happened in the family, and Susanne ended up calling my folks in tears. They drove down to get her and brought her and her little dog home to live with them until Wayne got back. Susanne got pregnant, but at around five months she miscarried a baby boy that they named Charles Wayne after his daddy. To make a long story short, she and Wayne eventually divorced after several years, and we've never heard from her again.

While living in this house, Mom first got called to serve as Relief Society president. The women took turns having Relief Society during the week at each other's houses because we didn't have our own church building. Mom was a great president and worked so hard at doing a good job. There were many ups and downs and personality clashes amongst some of the members, but Mom just pushed ahead and did her very best.

The church in Wooster was just a small branch with no building. We first met in the Seventh Day Adventist church because they didn't need it on Sunday since they went to church on Saturday. After that, our little branch moved to the High School and met in the band room. During all this time we all were trying to make money to buy property to build the first phase of our church building. Our little branch was assessed a certain percentage of the cost of the building, and the Church headquarters would pay the rest.

Our branch got a contract to sell tickets and clean the grandstand at the County Fair every summer for several summers. Mom would go during the day and help at the ticket booths, and late at night after the

Dutch colonial home at 734 North Grant in Wooster, Ohio.

fair had closed for the day whole families from our branch would go down with our tank vacuum cleaners and brooms and clean out the grandstands. We would be there until the wee hours of the morning, blowing the trash down from the top to the bottom and sweeping it all up into garbage bags. Night after night we'd do it for a week to earn money for land for our church.

We finally were able to purchase property after a few years, but then we had to earn money for the building. We still did our jobs at the county fair every summer, but we also planted our church property in strawberries and harvested those to sell to make more money. Finally we had saved up enough money for the first phase. Mom and Dad were right in the thick of all this and much more to help grow the tiny branch in Wooster, Ohio. They worked hard and accepted callings whenever asked.

A couple of years after moving to Wooster, Mom and Dad found another house to rent at 347 North Grant Street. It was sort of an arts and crafts house and had pretty oak trim and built-ins throughout the downstairs. In the basement was a dryer that the landlord said we could have if dad wanted to fix it. He fixed it, and it was the first time Mom had a dryer and didn't have to hang up clothes outside to dry. While living in this house, they celebrated their 25th wedding anniversary. Dad asked me to prepare a meal and send out invitations to their friends to come celebrate with them. I tried to keep it a secret, but I'm sure Mom knew something was up. It's hard to keep a shrimp aspic a secret while it's covered with paper towels in the fridge. I made individual meatloaves, which bubbled over in the oven, so they all had a not-so-nice smoky flavor. Mom asked me several times why in the world we said not to bring gifts on the invitations when we were providing an entire meal for everyone that came. Funny mother.

We moved one other time just down the street when Mom and Dad bought our pretty blue Dutch colonial house at 734 North Grant. Mom just loved that house. She loved everything about it—entryway, large living room with fireplace, a sun room off the living room, a dining room off the entry, and a cute little kitchen that she papered in bright orange and yellow flowery wall paper, and a breakfast nook off of that. She had a sewing room with wall-to-wall windows upstairs and three bedrooms. There was also a basement. Before we all moved in, we helped repaint everything. Susan was still at home at the time, and I worked full time during the week, so she and Mom made countless trips in the car to move everything from the old house to the new one. It was an exciting time.

Lots of important life events happened while Mom and Dad lived in Wooster. It was while living there that Susan and I eventually went off to college at BYU and in turn got married. Mom and Dad welcomed their first grandchildren while living in Wooster. They made lots of dear friends and grew in the Church. Dad made the decision to retire from Halliburton, where he had been employed for more than twenty years. He had accepted transfers time and again, and after he and Mom talked about it, he decided to accept a job at Harold Cook Inc., where they wouldn't be transferred and have to move again. He worked there for several years, and they continued with their square dance club that grew into quite a sizable club.

Anne, Harold, Rae, Hodge (dog), Wayne, and Susan visiting from Wooster in Anne and Jack's house in Bucyrus, Ohio.

Rigby, Idaho

After eight years in Wooster, Mom and Dad decided to make another move and join their daughters out west. Susan lived in Arizona, and I lived in Utah. Dad had gotten an offer to teach farm machinery mainte-nance at Ricks College. So in the fall of 1976 they sold their home in Wooster and bought a new home in Rigby, Idaho, just twenty minutes away from where Dad would be teaching at Ricks College. It was a major decision and a big move, but they were excited to make the changes and live closer to their children and grandchildren. Mom had always lived far away from her family after she married and moved to the states, so it was particularly important for her to be close to all of us. It's also interesting to note that the move to Idaho would bring her closer to Calgary than she'd ever been before during her whole married

Home in Rigby, Idaho.

life. Her parents had both died, but Jo, Gerrie, and Ruth still lived up there, and she was able to make a few trips home to see them.

Mom and Dad bought a brand new house on half an acre just outside of Rigby and moved in in November. When spring came, they started work on the outside and spent countless hours working in the yard over the next 23 years that they lived there. They had many truck loads of top-soil brought in, which they spread themselves. They planted grass, made flower beds, planted many trees front and back, and had a huge garden. Mom was able to have a big raspberry patch and enjoy raspberries like she did when she was a little girl back at home in Calgary.

All of Mom and Dad's grandchildren and some of their great-grandchildren have happy memories visiting their grandparents in Rigby, of picking raspberries and peas in the garden, sitting with their grandparents on the deck shelling and eating peas. Such happy, happy memories. Mom worked so hard making fun memories for her grandchildren. She would have them come for visits just for the fun of it, and they'd do fun things together.

For a while Mom had a job at a fabric store in Rigby, but when John asked if he could come visit and she had to tell him she had to work, she decided it was much more important for her to be with her grandchildren than it was for her to work, so she quit.

She had spent most of her paychecks in the fabric store while working there and had quite an amazing stash of fabrics for clothes and quilts. Sometimes when Susan and I were there visiting, she'd take us into her sewing room, open up the white metal cupboard, and show us the stacks and stacks of different folds of fabrics and patterns she had ready for future use.

Speaking of quilts, Mom took up quilting while she lived in Rigby and made a few beautiful quilts. I think she mostly did it to try and keep herself busy. She suffered from depression, and keeping busy helped her fight against it. She also took up counted cross stitching and tole painting and made so many beautiful things which have now been passed down through the family. Such treasures.

Mom tried her hand at a temporary job one fall just to make a little extra spending money. It was spud harvest, and she had heard of the good money she could make in two weeks sorting potatoes. She showed up one morning at the local spud cellar, lined up along the conveyer belt along with everyone else, and proceeded to sort the potatoes as they rolled by. By the time lunch time rolled around, she asked herself what the heck she was doing there and went to the farmer and quit. Sorting spuds in a dark, stinky spud cellar was not her cup of tea.

After a while she and dad decided that they had better buy burial plots in the cemetery down the road. For years after they got their plots we'd drive past the cemetery, and she'd laugh and say that's where she was going to be buried—in the Pioneer Cemetery wearing a pair of high-top tennis shoes. She had a great sense of humor. That's where she and Dad are buried now, but we didn't send her off in white high-top tennis shoes. Oh, how we miss them and all the good times.

One summer Mom had two of her granddaughters come stay with her for a week or so—Rachel and Erin. She helped them make baby quilts for their "hope chests." They went to the store and chose out their own fabric, and she helped them put their quilts together. Rachel still has hers.

While the girls were there, Grandma Rae let them drive their little Volkswagen Beetle into town to the local grocery store. They weren't even old enough to have a permit! One of them drove clear into town

Garden in Rigby.

to the grocery store, and the other drove back home. They thought that Grandma was so cool to let them do that. What a fun grandma they had!

During the summers she'd work hours in the yard, planting beautiful flowers and then pulling weeds from all her flower beds. Heaven knows how many raspberries and green beans she picked from their garden, or ears of corn. Then she would freeze the raspberries or make jars and jars of freezer jam and can jars and jars of green beans that she shared with her children, and she'd freeze corn on the cob. We enjoyed many a wonderful meal made from all the produce from their garden. Mom and Dad were such hard workers. I don't think they ever sat still during the summer except for an occasional short nap.

Mom took up genealogy while living in Rigby and spent countless hours at the genealogy library researching family names. She was able to go back several generations on several of her family lines. A couple of times when she and Dad went on road trips back to Ontario where her father's family came from, they'd walk through cemeteries looking for family members. She paid a genealogist in Yorkshire, England, to help find some of her ancestors, but I don't think she was ever successful.

Mom had taken piano lessons as a young girl and decided at the age of 65 to buy a piano and take lessons again. She was pretty proud of herself for trying to learn at such a late age. She practiced and practiced and learned to play "Rendezvous," which she just loved.

We loved to listen to Mom tell the story about the time she was dusting the furniture. She was just dusting away and came upon a wad of chewed gum sitting on the piano, so she just popped it into her mouth with the other gum she had in there. I guess she figured it wasn't Dad's, so she might as well enjoy it. After rolling it around in her mouth for a few minutes and trying to figure out why it wasn't getting soft, she spit it into her hand and looked at it. Lo and behold, it was Dad's hearing aid—covered in gum! She hurried and tried to get the outside cleaned off and then got a straight pin to dig all the gum out of holes. When she was done she put it back where she found it and went on her merry way. Later on Dad put his hearing aid back in but wondered why he couldn't hear out of it. He was talking to Mom about it, and she sheepishly confessed to what she had done. He ended up taking it in to be repaired. We never could figure out why Mom would pick up a chewed piece of gum and pop it in her mouth in the first place. Funny, funny Mom.

A couple of weeks each summer Susan and I would plan to take all eight of our kids up to Rigby and stay with Mom and Dad. Mom was always so excited to have us come. She'd cook and bake for us, and we'd have the best meals. Susan and I got to sleep in in the mornings, and when we got up we'd join everyone out on the deck and have breakfast. The kids had great fun playing in their backyard and digging in their garden. One year Dad built a go-cart, and boy did they all have fun on that. Round and round the backyard they'd speed. By the time we left to go back home, there were ruts in the grass all around the perimeter of the backyard where the kids had run the go-cart. Eventually, Dad gave the go-cart to the boys next door. Our kids were sorely disappointed when they found out.

Family in front of barn in Rigby, about 1985. Front row: *John, Megan, Rebekah, Erin, Rachel, Shannon.* Middle row: *Rae, Matt, Steve.* Back row: *Jack, Anne, Wayne, Harold, Don, Susan holding baby Carrie.*

The main thing we did during our summer visits was go to Rigby Lake every afternoon. First we'd have lunch, with Susan and I slapping together sandwiches in an assembly line fashion, and then about an hour after we ate, we'd all pile into Susan's van and Dad's pickup with inner tubes, water floaties, and lots of towels. We'd get our spot on the sandy beach and set up shop. The kids would run out into the lake, and Susan, Mom, and I would park our lawn chairs in the sand and break out the peanut M&Ms or orange slices. We'd sit there for hours watching the kids swim and popping M&Ms. One year all three of us got embroidery floss cases, so we spent most of our time rewinding the different colored flosses onto individual cards that fit in the cases. That was during our counted cross stitch phase. So many happy memories at Rigby Lake.

When Dad died on June 11, 2016, we went up to the Pioneer Cemetery to bury him, and afterward the whole family met at Rigby Lake, where we shared a picnic lunch provided by Dad's ward and shared

Harold built this deck and pergola with the help of family members.

Matt and Megan, grandchildren, with the go-cart.

happy memories of times past. I know Mom and Dad were both there with us. Since then my family has managed to meet there for a few hours once each summer to splash around and have a little picnic. Someone always brings peanut M&Ms and orange slices to share, and someone always leaves a small bag of peanut M&Ms on Mom's grave. Oh, what happy memories we all have of Grandma and Grandpa.

Missions

About a year after Dad retired from teaching at Ricks College, Mom decided they should go on a mission. They sent in their papers and received their mission call a few weeks later. They would be serving in the Indiana Indianapolis Mission for 18 months. They got their affairs in order and made arrangements for Wayne to live in and take care of the their house while they were gone. They were able to have their own car there in Indiana, so they drove down to Provo to the MTC (Missionary Training Center), where they learned what they needed to know to serve as missionaries. After being there for a few weeks, they left to drive cross country to Indiana. Mom and Dad made friends easily and made

Harold and Rae just before their mission to Indiana.

lots of new friends in the mission field. They enjoyed their mission, and Mom kept track of it in their daily mission journal. If anyone would like to read through those, both Susan and I have one for each of their missions. After serving the people in their mission for 18 months, they headed home. I'm pretty sure they took some detours on the way back and saw some interesting sites. The kids and grandkids met up at their house in Rigby before they got back and worked at cleaning up their yard and trimming a few trees. We were so excited for them to be back.

A few years later they decided to serve another mission. They wanted to go out of the country and would be gone two years. They were thrilled when they found out they would be going to Zaire, Africa. So far away! In the MTC they started learning to speak French, since that's what the people of Zaire spoke. After a few weeks they were ready to go, and off they went to Africa! They absolutely loved serving there. They loved the people with all their hearts, and the people loved them right back. They had a nice place to live that was surrounded by a concrete wall, as there were safety factors that had to be taken into consideration. They had a Land Rover to drive, but sometimes that would only get them so far, and they'd have to get out to walk along dusty paths and through the brush to get to the people's houses. They spent many hours sitting on chairs out in the dirt yards of the people they were visiting, talking to them about the church as the children played and the chickens and goats scratched around in the dirt. Everywhere they went, they took

Harold in Zaire with the ward clerk and the first counselor in the elders quorum. The wall surrounds the Binza chapel for security.

wrapped candy in their pockets for the little dusty children who would come up to them grinning from ear to ear with their hands outstretched, saying "Bonbon? Bonbon?"

Mom and Dad were in Zaire for nine months when one day Susan called me and said she had received a call from someone with a CB radio who had received a message from our dad saying "We are in a safe asylum." She called me and let me know. What the heck did that mean? We hadn't heard anything on the news about anything happening where they lived. I called Jack, who knew people in the missionary department at the Church headquarters. He called them, and through them we found out that the missionaries in Zaire had been evacuated under military protection because of civil unrest. We learned that they had been taken to the American Embassy, flown to Germany, and then flown on to Ft. Lauderdale, Florida, where they would remain for the rest

Rae with Meyango at his baptism in Zaire.

of their mission. Mom and Dad later told us that they could only take one suitcase, so they had to leave most everything they owned there. They couldn't even say goodbye to their friends and the members of their little branch. Mom decided they could always get more clothes, so they filled their suitcases with all the souvenirs they had been collecting. They left instructions for all the things they had to leave behind to be given to their friends in the little branch there. They always felt so bad that they couldn't even say goodbye to anyone. They were just scooped up and taken to the American Embassy with armed guards hanging from the running boards of the Land Rover.

It was while they were serving the rest of their mission in Florida that they met another convert to the Church, Steve Jenkins. They became great friends and enjoyed going over to his house with all the Elder missionaries for one of his famous fish fries with delicious hush puppies. He had taken all the Elder missionaries under his wing, and they all loved him. Later, after Mom and Dad had come home at the end of their mission, Steve moved to Salt Lake City. He was like a second son to them, and he called them Mom and Pop.

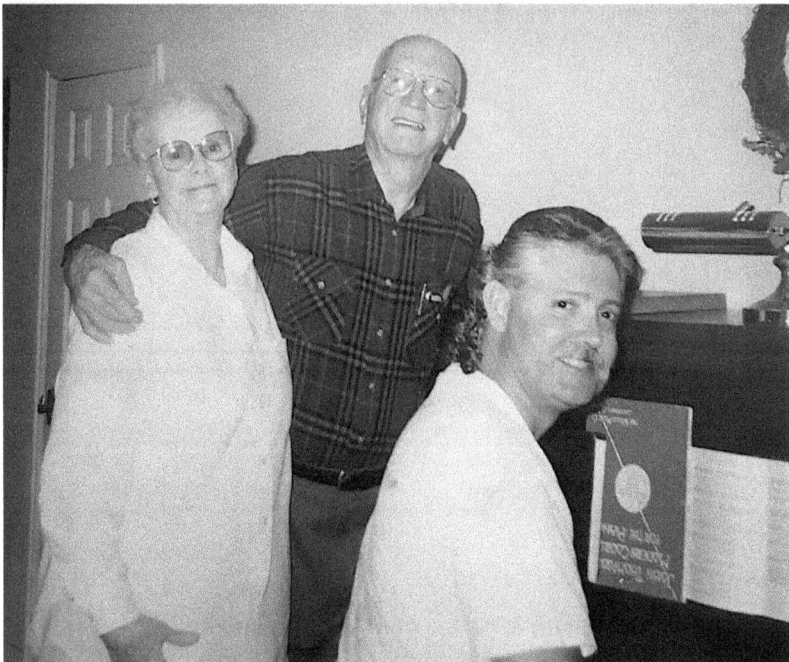

Rae, Harold, and Steve Jenkins at the piano.

After serving two missions, Mom and Dad decided that they'd like to work at the Idaho Falls temple as ordinance workers. They got up at 4:00 on the mornings that they served and worked an eight-hour shift. They may have done more than one shift a week, but whatever it was they just loved it. After their shift they'd often eat lunch downstairs in the temple cafeteria. Afterward, they'd come home, change clothes, and have a nap.

Mom and Dad loved to take road trips and spent hours and hours planning their next one. They'd travel to see friends from all the different places they had lived—New Mexico, Kentucky, Ohio. Dad had distant family that lived in eastern Kentucky, and they met them and visited with them for a few days. They saw the old Vance homestead and meandered through the old Vance cemetery. Mom had a brother that lived in Toronto, so they'd go to visit him. While they were there, they'd visit the old cemeteries around St. Mary's, Ontario, and look for Setterington and Uren gravestones and take pictures that she tucked in with the corresponding genealogy file back at home. They'd be gone for weeks at a time. They loved to travel.

Since we're talking about traveling, maybe this is a good place to tell about the times after we joined the church and Susan and I were still living at home with Mom and Dad and we'd all go on a road trip together. Mom would always bring a tote bag along with the latest book or two she was reading—always church books or self-improvement books, but mostly church books. This was the time that she literally had a captured audience with us all in the car rolling down the road, so many is the time she'd say, "Just let me read you this short paragraph," or "Let me just read you these few lines. It won't take long." We'd all groan because we knew it would end up being way longer than she said it would. She was always so enthusiastic about the things she read and the new things she learned.

And since we're talking about church books, this seems like a good place to tell about the time she and Dad were visiting at my house after I was married and living in West Valley. She, Jack and I were in the living room one afternoon, and she and Jack were talking about church things and books they'd been reading. And she said something to me that I can't remember now, but my answer to her was "I don't like to read church books." She then turned to Jack and said in all seriousness, "Jack, don't you think there's something wrong with someone that doesn't like to read church books?" I don't remember what Jack's response was, and I can't remember if I had one, but I do remember not being very happy about her comment.

Last move

After living 23 years in Rigby, Mom and Dad decided they were going to move down to West Valley City, Utah, so they could be closer to me and my family. This was early in the year. They sold their house, and before they had to move out, they came down to West Valley and we went around looking at houses. They finally decided on a little house down the street from where I lived on Marsha Drive. Dad paid cash for it, and they went back to Rigby to pack and get ready to move. Both of them worked hard at packing box after box after box until most everything was ready to go. They had a lot of stuff they didn't want to move, so they decided to have a garage sale—in January! Susan and I went up to help them, and they did pretty well, all except for their long Early

American couch. I think Dad had priced it at $50 or so, but it just would not sell. I told him to lower the price to $25 and some little Hispanic family would snatch it up. About five minutes after he changed the price, in walks a little Hispanic family who were thrilled to have a new couch that they could afford and paid the $25. It was kind of funny.

While Mom and Dad were still getting ready for the big move up in Rigby, my family and I were down getting their new house ready for them to move into. We cleaned and painted and put new shelf liner in all their cupboards. We wanted it ready for them to move right in.

Wayne, Susan, and I had all chipped in to pay for a moving company to move all of Mom and Dad's stuff, so the day before the move Jack and I went up to help. It took forever, but finally after it had gotten dark and the moving truck was gone and we were done vacuuming and cleaning, we got in our cars and drove all the way back down to West Valley. We were exhausted when we finally got there four hours later.

The next day Mom and Dad moved into their new home on Marsha Drive, and it was so much fun to have them living just down the street. We'd go often to visit, and they'd come up often to our house. I think Mom loved it most of all—to be close to her family and be able to watch her little great-grandchildren grow up.

They were both close to eighty years old when they moved this last time, and they had slowed down quite a bit. Dad still liked to keep busy, and he restored two more Volkswagen Beetles in his garage. Mom loved driving those little Beetles. She was darn good with a stick shift!

Shortly after moving to West Valley City, Wayne and Susan moved to town. Now all our family was within just a few minutes of each other. Mom and Dad were thrilled to have our family so close together again. We enjoyed lots of get-togethers at Anne and Jack's and picnics in their backyard. We even celebrated their 50th wedding anniversary back there with steak and shrimp and a special cake made by a local bakery. We all loved being together, and I know Mom and Dad especially loved being surrounded by all their loved ones.

They continued to take trips for a few years, and then Mom got to where she just couldn't travel like that anymore. I think they went up to Rigby a couple of times to see their friends there. Mom slowly grew more feeble in both body and mind. The doctor thought that she could possibly have Alzhiemer's, but I really never thought she did. She became forgetful but never forgot who we all were or what our names

Harold, Anne, and Rae with baby Abbie, November 26, 1995. Abbie and her twin sister, Brynn, were Harold and Rae's first great-grandchildren.

Harold and Rae on their 50th wedding anniversary.

were. She continued to require more and more help with day-to-day functions, and Dad was right there beside her helping her and taking care of her. Finally, on May 19, 2006, she passed quietly away at 5:00 in the morning.

Such a wonderful person. She tried her hardest in all that she did. She was the most caring and loving mother, wife, and grandmother. Her whole married life she never missed a day getting up to fix breakfast for her husband and children and always had a hot meal on the table when Dad arrived home after work. Even after we three children were married and on our own, she continued to get up every morning with Dad, fix him breakfast, pack his lunch, and send him off to work. Every evening she'd have dinner waiting for him. After he retired, they'd get up together in the morning for breakfast, and later in the evening she'd have dinner ready for the both of them. She took care of us all until she couldn't anymore. Then we all took care of her. It was such an honor and privilege to be able to do that for her, after she had taken such excellent care of all of us her whole life long. Our dear, dear mother.

PATRIARCHAL BLESSING

THE CHURCH OF JESUS CHRIST OF LATTER-DAY SAINTS

Cleveland _____ STAKE   No. 79 __

August 25, 1968 _____ Westlake _____ Ohio
DATE   CITY   STATE

A BLESSING given by Frank Alan Woodbury _____ Patriarch, upon the head of

Allie Rae Williams _____ son/daughter of
WRITE NAME IN FULL

Harold Aubrey Setterington __ and __ Mabel Alice Rogers
FATHER'S NAME IN FULL   MOTHER'S MAIDEN NAME

born March 25, 1921 __ at __ Calgary, Alberta, Canada
DATE   CITY   COUNTY   STATE

Dear Sister Allie Rae Williams, by the authority of the Holy Melchizedek Priesthood I place my hands upon your head, according to your desire, and seal upon you a patriarchal blessing for your enrichment and understanding of the purpose of your earth life.

Dear Sister Williams, you are one of the chosen servants of our Heavenly Father, having been born to the earth in the royal lines of Israel even through the tribe of Joseph and Ephraim. And if you are faithful and true to the covenants which you have made at the time of your baptism you shall receive all of those blessings which our Heavenly Father in His great mercy desires for you to receive, even the blessings of health and strength and joy and happiness in this life, and exaltation at the side of your companion in the next life. Sister Williams, you were highly favored as a choice spirit in the presence of our Heavenly Father in the spirit world before you came to this earth, and because of your diligent spirit and your desire for justice and truth in the life before, you were granted the opportunity of coming to the earth and being born at a time and under such conditions that you could share the blessings of the gospel.

Your Heavenly Father has been merciful unto you by persisting in providing circumstances that would help you and your family to receive this gospel message. And you besides your husband have a great responsibility to seek after the records of your ancestors that these ancestors who will partake or who have partaken of the gospel message and accepted it may have the ordinance work done for them in the temple so that they may go on unto perfection. Sister williams, it is most important for you to bear your testimony and to exemplify your sweet spirit among those with whom you associate; not only with those who are not members of the church, but with the members as well, for you have the ability to strengthen the testimony of other sisters, and as you are called in various capacities to serve the Lord, your spirit will be the means of strengthening the bonds of love for the other sisters of the church, that they might be strengthened and spared many difficulties because of your wonderful influence. You will have the opportunity of adding great strength to your children and if you will exemplify this same spirit of testimony, your daughters will regard you highly and will desire with all their hearts to keep the commandments of God so that they too may be worthy one day of the great blessings which He desires for them to receive.

I pronounce upon you the blessings of health and strength that you may have a long life upon this earth to perform your duties and responsibilities and your children will be kind to you throughout your life.

I seal you up against the power of the destroyer that you may have power to overcome every obstacle and temptation that would hinder you from the accomplishment of your life's mission and I seal you up to come forth in the morning of the first resurrection with your husband, providing you both shall comply with the requirements of this sealing ordinance, to come forth in the morning of the first resurrection clothed with glory and immortality and eternal life. These blessings I seal upon your head by the power of the Priesthood which I hold and in the name of our Lord and Savior, Jesus Christ, Amen.

Frank Alan Woodbury, Patriarch
Cleveland Stake

Life Sketch, Given by Rebekah Anderson, Granddaughter, at Rae's Funeral Services

One of the many stories my grandmother told me as I was growing up was the story of the day she was born. It was on Good Friday, during a snow storm on March 25, 1921 in Calgary, Alberta, Canada. She was the third of five children to be born to Mable Alice Rogers and Harold Aubrey Setterington. She had one older brother, Jack, an older sister, Ruth, and two younger sisters, Jo and Gerrie. We have all spent hours listening to the stories of her life at home in Calgary, her family and relatives, and feel we have come to know them all even though we have never met. I know that she is having a great reunion with all these loved ones and reliving all the old stories. She has always said she had a wonderful childhood and was raised in an ideal home. She had wonderful memories of visits with her family to the Cave and Basin, Banff and Lake Louise, and longer trips back east to Detroit, Leamington, and St. Mary's to visit family members from both her mother and father's side of the family. She spent summer months swimming with her brother, sisters, and friends in the river not far from her house. They sat on the front steps every day in the summer, dressed in their swimming suits and holding their towels, anxiously awaiting the end of the hour their mother had them wait after eating lunch so they wouldn't get cramps while swimming. When the hour was up they shot off the porch and raced to the river, where they swam for hours. The winter was spent walking to school in subzero weather, ice skating, and tobogganing.

She had the typical Canadian education until the age of 16 when she attended the Catholic convent in Red Deer. From those two years have come colorful stories of austere living; strict nuns; washing face and hands in washbowls of cold water after breaking the thin layer of ice off the top; cold, congealed porridge for breakfast; and long, cold walks in the snow. She kept in touch for over sixty years with some of her classmates at the convent and a few of the nuns.

She met my grandpa when she was 25. They were introduced on a blind date while he was stationed in Edmonton during World War II. They had a whirlwind romance and were married July 31, 1946, in her parents' living room. Because of her great love for my grandpa, she left her beloved Calgary and family to move with him to Oklahoma. Grandma told us many stories of their early married life. They lived through some challenging situations, but it drew them closer together, and their love grew because of it. Two years later, on January 8, 1948, their first and only son, Wayne, was born in Oklahoma City.

In 1950 the three of them moved to Hays, Kansas, where my mother, Anne, was born a year later. When she was just a few months old their family moved yet again, this time to Garden City, Kansas, where they lived just a year and a half. Their next move, sometime between 1953 and 1954, was to Borger, Texas. This is where their youngest daughter, Susan, was born. When she was two years old they all moved to Farmington, New Mexico. They lived seven years there, had close friends, and spent many happy hours square dancing, playing cards, and going on family campouts every other weekend during the summer to their favorite camping spot up La Plata Canyon. There they joined with their friends and their families in hikes, or just enjoyed sitting and visiting by the river.

It was while they were living in Farmington that they were introduced to the church by two missionaries that came knocking at their door. Even after taking the discussions they were not ready to accept the gospel, but they did stay in touch with these first two missionaries for many years. In 1964 they moved to Henderson, Kentucky. Moving was always hard for Grandma, but the move to Henderson was especially hard for her. It was during this time that she was looking for comfort in her life. They had never been a church-going family but began attending the Bennett Memorial Methodist Church. It was around this same time that they started a square dance club in their basement. One of the couples that took square dance lessons from Grandpa was LDS. Because of Grandma and Grandpa's positive experience with the missionaries years before in New Mexico, they asked to have the missionaries come by for a visit. The family again took the missionary discussions. Grandma found what she had been searching for in the LDS Church and decided to be baptized. Grandpa talked to Wayne, Anne, and Susan and told them of Grandma's intentions. He said that they could all be baptized when Grandma got baptized, or if they weren't ready, he would wait to be baptized until they were ready. They decided that this was an important time for their family and were all baptized together as a family on March 16, 1967, and were later sealed together in the temple as an eternal family. It is because of Grandma's search for truth and meaning in her life that our family is sitting here today as an eternal family.

A while after their baptism they made yet another move—this time to Wooster, Ohio, where they lived nine years. It was while they lived there that their three children began to marry, move away, and have families of their own. In 1976 Grandpa was invited to teach at Ricks College, so they packed up their things and made one more move to a new home in Rigby, Idaho, where they spent the best 23 years of their married lives Their home in Rigby is where all of us grandchildren have so many memories of happy times at Grandma Rae's and Grandpa Harold's— eating Grandma's special recipe for applesauce with her tiny applesauce spoons, long days spent at Rigby Lake, Grandma's famous PBF, riding the go-cart Grandpa made us in the backyard, picking raspberries and peas from their garden, and playing pingpong and making tents under the pingpong table.

After Grandpa retired from Ricks College they served two missions— one to the Indianapolis Indiana Mission from 1987 to 1989, and a second mission to Zaire, Africa. They began this part of their second mission in February 1991 and were able to only stay nine months when they were evacuated. They had come to love the people there and always felt bad that they weren't able to say goodbye to their friends. The rest of their mission was spent in the Florida Ft. Lauderdale mission. It was there they came to know and love Steve Jenkins. He has since moved to Salt Lake City and has become like a member of our family.

In the year 2000 Grandma and Grandpa decided to make the last move of their lives and come to Utah, where they could be closer to their family. At that time they moved down the street from my mother, Anne. A short time later Susan and Wayne moved to town. Grandma and Grandpa now lived within one or two minutes of all their children. Grandma, who was never able to live close to her family once she was married, and could only go back to Calgary for brief visits, was now surrounded by her own family. Family was always the most important thing to Grandma, and as she reached the last moments of her life, she was surrounded by those who loved her most—here and in the next life. She left this life in the loving arms of her two daughters and was welcomed into the loving arms of her family and friends who have passed on before her—to those that we knew meant so much to her, because we as her husband, children, grandchildren, and great grandchildren have had the great honor and privilege of many times sitting at her side as she told us the stories of how their lives and hers entwined. Now she's in the spirit world with them sitting at her side, telling them stories about those of us left behind here, and how much we mean to her and how much she loves us. Grandma has left behind a wonderful legacy of love and caring, and we have been so very blessed to be a part of her life. We love you Grandma.

LAST DAYS, WRITTEN BY ANNE LYON, DAUGHTER, A FEW DAYS AFTER THE FUNERAL

I want to write this down before it becomes a dim memory. My mother, Rae Williams, passed away Friday, May 19, 2006, at 5:00 in the morning. These are my memories of that day and the days leading up to it.

Mom had been diagnosed with Alzheimer's a year or so after she and Dad moved down here to Salt Lake City from Rigby, Idaho, where they had previously lived for twenty-three years. Mom had always wanted to be down here close to me and my children, but not until 2001 did they make the move. Dad always wanted to stay in Idaho, but he was foreseeing the day when both he and Mom would need help as they got older. At the time of their move Mom was 80 and Dad was 79. They actually moved into their new house down the street from me the day of his birthday.

So Mom very slowly grew worse. Sometimes I wondered if she really had Alzheimer's, or was it the effect of dementia brought on by a few of the mini-strokes she had after moving here. I still don't know. If it was Alzheimer's, we were blessed that it didn't progress into the horror stories you hear about others and their families that had to deal with it. Dad and I took Mom to a geriatiric specialist when we noticed she was asking the same thing over and over in just a few minutes of time. At first I just thought she was trying to keep the conversation going. She always asked lots of questions, just not the same ones repeatedly. She also laughed about not being able to find where she left the car keys or her checkbook. Once a lady in their ward got mad at her because Mom said she would pick her up for a senior sister's luncheon and she forgot. Mom said she never made those arrangements, and at the time

I figured she was right. Now that I look back on it, I think it was just the beginning of Alzheimer's.

Dad took care of Mom until the day she died. She gradually quit doing things around the house. Following a recipe became too difficult. Dad would read it to her, and she would follow his instructions, but after a while that ended. It was harder and harder for her to get around. She fell going up the stairs to one of the ladies she visit taught and hit her face. She looked awful—all black and blue and yellow. Gradually she started using a cane around the house, and then Dad would take her out in her wheelchair. Then she needed a walker around the house. Dad got her a motorized chair that would lift her up to a near standing position, where she would hold on to her walker to get around the house. He bought a used minivan and redid the passenger seat so that it would rotate out to face the open door, then pull out to hang slightly over the door jam, and she could step up onto a step that he could pull out from under the edge of the car. For a couple of years he would take her on outings that way, taking the wheelchair in the back of the van. They'd go to lunch or dinner and maybe hang out at the mall. It was hard on my Dad's knees, but he was happy to do it all for Mom.

Physically she became less and less able to do things for herself. I think if she had had normal brain function she would've done more, but her excuse was that she was 83, then 84, and finally 85, and people that age didn't have to do what they didn't want to do because they had earned that right from living such a long life. So use it or lose it became true in her situation. Her personality changed. She was very childish. She never forgot who anyone was. She always knew everyone who came to visit. That was such a blessing. She became obsessed about ice. We bought ice trays that made little miniature marshmallow-sized ice cubes, and Dad made dozens of trips a day getting her ice. She became obsessed about popcorn for a while. She wouldn't be hungry for lunch or dinner many times because she was full of popcorn. Funny things like that. She loved to look through all the many different catalogs that would come in the mail—especially around Christmastime. One time she ordered $500 worth of cloisonne from the Smithsonian catalog. Everyone got cloisonne gifts for a couple of years after that. They're treasures now.

Mom was always so happy when I visited. I tried to go down every other day or so. She was particularly happy when Rebekah and her children came. She loved Abbie, Brynn, and Sam. I'm so happy she got to hold Rebekah's fourth baby, Lydia, born April 12. We have pictures of that. She couldn't thank us enough for coming to visit, or for what we did to help out while we were there.

For a while Susan and I took turns taking meals over to Mom and Dad. We each had two days of the week, then we slowed it down to one day a week each. Finally Dad had us stop it altogether. We never knew if it was because Mom didn't like the food, or Dad didn't like it. I thought it was because I took too much food over, so they'd have leftovers on the days we didn't take in a meal. So, for whatever reason, we just quit the meals. Once in a while we'd take over leftovers, or I'd bake cookies or bread for them. I never knew quite what to do about helping around the house. I didn't want to just rush in and take over. Once in awhile Susan, Rebekah, and I would go over and give their place a good cleaning. Periodically I'd gather up all of Mom's old magazines and catalogs and sneak them out to the garbage

Mom never said much about having Alzheimer's. Of course, she probably didn't remember she had it! Dad had written a few of their friends and Mom's sisters and told them, and when she found out she was so mad at him. A couple of times the last few months, I would help her into bed at night, and she would say, "I don't feel right." I'd ask her if she was sick, and she'd say "No. Something's just not right in my head." I felt badly about that.

In February of 2006, Dad had knee replacement surgery on his left knee. He was in the hospital and the rehab center for nearly three weeks. Wayne, Susan, and I made up a daily calendar for the time Dad was away from home. We each knew when we were "on duty," and it worked out exceptionally well. When Dad came home, we modified the schedule some, but we still helped out a lot.

Mom's younger sister, Jo, died in April. That was so hard on Mom. She would just break down and cry. She said she couldn't quit thinking about her. She'd ask us if Jo was okay. I always told her she was better off than we were—she didn't have any pain, and she could breathe and get around. I had to tell her that many times. It was after Jo's death that Mom started going downhill more quickly. She lost her appetite. She'd eat a pretty good breakfast—for her anyway. Dad always served her half of a grapefruit after she got up in the morning and shuffled out to the wing-back chair in the living room. After that, she had her morning pills and two pieces of bacon and toast with jam. Sometimes he'd give her waffles and syrup instead of toast and jam. She got up so late in the morning that she was never ready for lunch at noon. I think many times Dad just waited until supper for her next meal. She'd probably have some popcorn. She ate a lot of Werther's hard candy, too.

Around the time that my Aunt Jo died, I had two granddaughters born: Lydia Anne, born to Rebekah and Rob on April 12, and Sage Vivian Lyon, born to my son Matt and his wife, Yvonne, on April 25. I had already told Mom and Dad that I wouldn't be able to be come down to their house as much during April and some of May because I would be going to help take care of the new babies and their families. In May I went up to Matt and Yvonne's in St. Anthony, Idaho, and stayed a week. When I came back, I went down to see Mom and Dad. The first thing I noticed when I walked into their family room was that Mom's wheelchair was there. I asked what the reason was for that, and Dad said that Mom couldn't walk very well with her walker anymore, so he moved her around the house in that. She had to go to the bathroom right after I got there, so I helped her into her wheelchair. She had such a hard time getting turned around from standing up by her recliner to sitting in the wheelchair, and then she had an even harder time getting out of the wheelchair at the door of the bathroom and walking the few feet to the toilet. She had declined so much in that one week I was gone. I helped her with a shower while she was in there, and she could hardly lift her foot the three or four inches it took to clear the edge of the shower. She barely made it from the toilet to the shower chair, which was just a couple of feet away. She was deathly afraid of falling. Susan got her to walk from the family room back to her bed the next evening, but it took a lot of encouragement. That was the last shower she had.

Dad and Wayne took her to see the geriatric doctor a few days later. I don't know what she saw, but I'm pretty sure she didn't say anything to Dad and Wayne. She just said she would call a hospice care service for us and get that started. They started coming on May 12. Mom was staying in bed most of the day. Susan and I would sometimes convince her to get up and move into the TV room. Helping her get up and work her way around the bed and into her wheelchair by the bedroom door and finally into her recliner in the TV room was a major undertaking. Then we'd have to reverse the procedure to help her into bed at night. She was always afraid we were going to drop her when helping her out of her wheelchair, or laying her down in bed. We never did. It got so that we had to bring the portapotty to her because she couldn't make it into the bathroom anymore. We finally got a hospital bed. We got it on Wednesday, May 17, and we had her moved to the hospice care center on Thursday. She passed away Friday, May 19, at 5:00 in the morning. I just felt like she knew she was going and didn't want to prolong the process. She took a nosedive every day that last week or so.

On Mother's Day, May 14, we took flowers and chocolates to her and kind of left them on her bed and on the dresser so she could see them. We set her cards there, too. Susan gave her a box of Russell Stover chocolates. I think she had a bite out of one chocolate. I took my flower arrangement over to her in the morning before church because my children and grandchildren would go over when they came to my house for dinner. I knew it would be really hard and sad for them, and it was. Mom had gone downhill so much. All of Susan's children called after Susan had told them it would probably be the last Mother's Day she would be with us. Matt called her later in the evening. So she was able to visit with all her family. No one said anything about it maybe being the last Mother's Day. I don't think any of them thought it would be the last time they would be able to talk to her or see her.

I don't remember what day it was, but one evening I was there talking to Mom, sitting on the edge of their king-sized bed. She wanted me to reread the card she had gotten from Karen Vance, a friend of theirs from many years back. In the card, Karen told Mom how much she admired her and all the great things Mom had done. Mom just wanted to hear that again. She never felt like she had done anything so spectacular in her life, and she just liked to hear from people about the good things she did. I don't think any of us did that like we should have. I feel bad about that now.

Back to moving Mom into a hospital bed—I had gotten a call from Dad Tuesday morning at 6:30 saying he had gotten Mom on the portapotty but couldn't get her off by himself. There was so little room in their bedroom with the dresser, chest of drawers, and a king-sized bed, there just wasn't enough room to maneuver. Anyway, I got dressed and hurried down the street and helped get her back in bed, thinking the whole time about what Mom used to say about the morning, just after getting out of bed, was when your back was the weakest. I've had back problems the past few years and knew that lifting and moving Mom around was not going to do great things for my back. She had gotten to the point that she just couldn't make her legs and feet work. It was like she had lost the ability to tell them what to do, and she just didn't have any strength left. We got her back in bed and comfortable, and I went back home. About 10:00 or so, Dad called again for help getting her onto the portapotty, so I went back down. The hospital bed was going to be delivered that afternoon, so we thought we ought to move Mom back into her recliner in the TV room while we had her up. That took us nearly an hour to move her about 25 feet, from one room right around the corner to the other room and into her chair. I was lifting her and trying to turn her to sit in her wheelchair, which was sitting in the doorway of her bedroom, when I felt a sharp pain in my back. I got her situated in her chair and told Dad that I wouldn't be able to lift Mom anymore. I called Jack to come down and help get her into her recliner. He came right down, and just as he arrived, the hospice girl came that was going to give her her first bed bath. She just lifted her up, turned her, and set her in her chair with one sweeping movement. She was a life saver. So Mom had her first bedbath in her chair.

Later on, Wayne and Jack moved the king-sized bed out of Mom and Dad's bedroom, then moved the dresser into the spare room, where there was a queen-sized bed that Dad was going to sleep in. I vacuumed and straightened things up. All the time Mom was calling from her chair in the TV room and asking us what we were doing and would she like her new bedroom with the new bed. Before the bed came, Dad and Wayne drove over to some store that sells home-care equipment and bought a lift to move Mom from the bed to the portapotty. They brought that home and figured out how it worked while the hospital bed men set up the new bed. Mom wanted to know what all the activity was about. I felt so sorry for her. As we were moving her into her "new room," she asked Wayne if she was going to be bedridden from now on, and he said "Yes, pretty much." I think with my heaving her around that morning and then hearing that she was going to be bedridden pretty much cinched it for her. She never said anything, but after looking back on it, I'm sure that's how she felt. I've always felt badly about having to heft her around like that to get her into her wheelchair. Looking back on it, Dad and I could've done a couple of things differently to make moving her easier on all three of us, but we were pretty much in a desperate situation. We had to get her out of the room so we could move the bed out, because the guys with the hospital bed wouldn't do it for us. We did the best we could at the time.

That evening, about dinner time, I called and left a message on Susan's cell phone. She was at work, and I had found the best way to get in touch with her was to leave a message on her cell phone, which she would get when she got out to her car after work. I said that we thought she probably ought to look at taking a leave of absence from her temple job on Wednesdays, so she'd be available the whole day to help Mom and Dad. Wednesday was her day off, and she worked at the temple from 5:00 A.M. and didn't get home until almost noon. It was the only day besides Sunday that she was available, and I just felt like I needed to have a day off. Poor Dad, he never got a day off. Susan called a little later in the evening, and I told her about the horrific day we had all spent, and she was surprised to hear about all of it. She said if she needed to, she would take a leave of absence from the temple—we'd wait and see how things were.

The next day was Wednesday. Susan and Wayne were over at Mom and Dad's most of the day. Wayne was teaching Susan how to use the lift. I went over later in the morning so I could learn too, and I couldn't believe how much Mom had changed. She had a kind of glazed look in her eyes. She was still talking to everyone, but not as much. Rebekah went over in the afternoon to clean the bathrooms, and Mom knew she was there and talked to her. Rebekah said the last thing she said to her as she was walking down the hall to leave and Mom called out to her and thanked her for all she did. That was Mom. She just couldn't thank you enough. That was the last time Mom talked to Rebekah and the last time Rebekah saw her alive.

Thursday. The hospice nurse was coming to check on Mom. The shower lady was coming to give her a bath. I went back to see Mom when I got there in the morning. Her eyes were half closed and glazed over. Her mouth was open, and she wasn't really able to talk very well because her mouth was so dried out from breathing. She didn't really talk—just sort of stared straight ahead with her eyes half open if she was awake. Mostly she was asleep. The nurse came and went and didn't really say much. The "shower girl" from Care Source came and gave Mom a bed bath. She couldn't believe how much she had changed since she was there a few days earlier. It was the last bath Mom had. It hurt her to be moved. I helped the shower girl kind of roll her onto her side, and Mom called out in pain to just be moved that much.

After the nurse and shower girl left, Wayne, Dad, and I talked about moving Mom to the hospice care center. We knew she didn't have long— maybe a few days or a week. We just didn't know. I told Dad we'd do whatever it was he wanted. He decided that Wayne would stay with Mom, and he and I would go over to Care Source, the only hospice care center in Utah. I drove us both over there, and we got a short tour. It was beautiful. So serene and peaceful. They said they could send their van over later in the afternoon. While we were in the room with the director and Dad was signing forms and writing a check, the director left for a few minutes. When she came back in, she said they could actually pick Mom up right then. Two very nice men (I forget their names) followed us in their van back home.

Wayne had stayed with Mom and said that while Dad and I were gone that he had pulled his chair up to sit close to Mom and told her what was going to happen and how much we all loved her. It was really sad to have the two men from Care Source come take Mom. Dad went into the TV Room and just sat there after helping to hold Mom's head up as they moved her from the bed to the gurney. We were all crying quietly, and the men from Care Source were so nice and sensitive. After getting Mom into their van, Wayne and Dad got in one car and I got in mine. We wanted to be there when Mom got there. We all got there about the same time and went in to see Mom and let her know we were there with her. They wanted to do an exam and get her settled in, so we waited out in the waiting room.

Care Source isn't like a hospital or nursing home. It's a place where people go to die, and the people that work there do everything they can to make that experience as nice as possible. The only thing that even remotely looks like a hospital in the individual rooms is a computer monitor on the wall. Any equipment they need they bring from some room down the hall. Actually, it isn't even a hall. All the rooms open up onto a common area that looks like a great, huge family room with nice furniture and a fireplace. It's very quiet and peaceful. In the rooms there's nice furniture and wooden blinds on the windows and a door that leads outside. The TV is in a big armoire instead of a black iron bracket hanging from the ceiling. There were nice table lamps and several comfortable chairs. The door leading outside from each room was wide enough so that if you wanted, you could take the patient outside to a beautifully landscaped area. We couldn't have asked for a nicer place for Mom. I'm so glad that Dad decided to have her be there for her last hours.

After spending a little time with Mom after she was situated, Dad and I left. Wayne stayed for a couple of more hours. I took Dad home, and I went back to my house. I think Susan had tried calling down at Mom and Dad's after we had taken Mom to Care Source, but of course no one was there to talk to her. She knew something out of the ordinary was up, so she called Jack, who told her what was going on. She was surprised that things had moved so quickly and that we had moved Mom. She left work early and went over to sit with Mom. I think Wayne had just barely left when she got there, so she wasn't by herself for very long, if at all.

While I was at home I called our children and let them know what was happening. John and Rachel decided that they'd go to see their grandma. Rebekah decided to stay home since she had just seen her the day before. She wanted to remember her the way she had last seen her. Rachel had had reservations to go to France for a few months and was due to fly out the next morning. I had asked Dad what he thought she should do, and it was his suggestion that she go by and say goodbye to Grandma and continue on with her plans. I'm sure that's what Mom would've wanted her to do too. Anyway, Jack and I picked up Dad and we all went back over to be with Mom. Rachel and John were there just barely before we got there. We all met in the parking lot. Of course, John and Rachel were sad and teary. It was a sad, sad time. I tried to prepare them for how much Mom had changed while we walked in. We took turns sitting by Mom, and her visiting teachers, Rosie and Michelle and Judy came by too. For a while I sat by Mom and held her hand. She was so hot. Rachel and John were there for about an hour. When Rachel went over to say goodbye, Mom roused when she heard me tell her Rachel was there. She said goodbye to Jack. You could barely understand her, but you knew she knew they were there. After everyone left, it was only Dad, Susan and I.

The doctor had been to see Mom shortly before we all got there and had talked to Susan. She said that it didn't look like Mom had a whole lot longer—maybe through the night. But seeing the pattern of how quickly things had been going, she thought she might not have more than a few hours. After everyone left, Susan needed to go home and do a few things and change her clothes. She took Dad back home. While they were gone, Wayne and Karen came by for an hour or so. Susan was gone quite a while and finally got back sometime after 10:00. Mom wasn't responsive while I was with her. I wet a wash cloth and wiped her face and lips.

When Susan came back, we sat by Mom's side until 1:00 or so and then decided to see if we could sleep. I knew I wouldn't be getting any sleep, but I reclined in the reclining chair we brought in from out in the sitting area. Susan made a bed out of the little fold-out bed in one of the chairs. We turned out the lights, and the only light in the room came from the blue screen of the computer monitor. The only sound was from the oxygen concentrating machine that provided oxygen for Mom and her breathing. We lay awake listening to any changes in her breathing. The nurse had told us some things to look for that would indicate that death was not too far away. Every once in a while I'd get up and go sit by mom and watch her in that blue light from the computer screen. At about 4:00 in the morning, her breathing started to get kind of rattley, and we called the nurse in. He raised the head of her bed up a little. Her breathing was changing some then too, and he said that she probably didn't have much longer. We should probably call Wayne and Dad. Susan did that at about 4:45 A.M., then went in to the bathroom. I stayed with Mom and talked with the nurse. He told me that sometimes the dying person just needs permission to go. I looked at Mom and thought that she didn't need to "labor" at dying anymore, and told her that if she was ready to go that she could, and that she had done such a good job. I told her to give our love to Maemo, Aunt Allie, and all the people she had told us so many stories about throughout our lives. By then Susan had come back, and we just kept telling her how much we loved her, held her hands, and stroked her head. Immediately after I had given her permission to leave, her breathing changed dramatically, and she was gone within just a few minutes. Susan and I both bent over her, and all three of us hugged, and Susan and I cried. Mom died at 5:00 A.M., Friday, May 19, 2006. I called Wayne, who was over at Dad's by then, and told him Mom had passed away.

As Susan and I sat by Mom's bed, we could see the sun just starting to come up and hear the birds chirping outside. I commented to Susan about it, and we decided to open the doors so that we could see better and hear the birds. It was pretty symbolic—a new day and new life.

Anyway, after the door had been open for just a minute or two, we could smell a skunk, and the smell kept getting stronger and stronger. We kind of looked at each other, there in the room with Mom, and I said quietly, "I think you'd better close the door." We laughed at that and remarked how Mom was probably getting a kick out of the situation too. It was something that she would've really appreciated the humor in.

The nurses came back in after a little while to clean Mom up, I guess. They just had us leave for a few minutes. When we came back in, they had opened the blinds and window, and everything was so peaceful. Shortly after, Wayne and Dad came. We were there for about half an hour more and then we left. I thanked the nurse that was with us through the night. Susan and I rode home in her car. We were going from about 2100 E. 4100 S. towards the West. Susan had a CD on. I think it might have been the Mormon Tabernacle Choir, and they were singing "Going Home" or something like that. The Oquirrh Mountains on the west side of the valley are usually kind of plain and ordinary looking, but that morning they looked majestic. The sunlight was reflecting off of them, and it looked just beautiful. I hadn't cried very much during the night, and I didn't cry very much when Mom died, but all the way home I cried and cried and cried. I told Susan it felt like my heart was broken. As we came down off the hill from the east side, I looked up in the sky in front of us, and there were three Canada geese flying together across the horizon, in front of the those beautiful Oquirrh Mountains, and I knew it was a message from Mom. She was letting us know that we three were still all together and would be forever. (Ten months later, as I was reading her personal history, I came to the part where she told about a dream she had when her father died. She wasn't able to go home for his funeral, but she had a dream about him and her family. In the end of the dream her dad said he had to go and got up to leave. As they looked off into the setting sun, with the sun's rays shining from behind the mountains, a bird was flying in those rays, until he flew over the mountain. She said she and her mother received a lot of comfort from that dream, and I feel like she was doing the same for me.)

Well, by the time Susan dropped me off at my house, I felt completely drained. Jack was waiting for me as I came into the house. I kind of fell apart then, too. We went upstairs, and I decided to have a nap. I think Jack called the children. I don't know how long I slept, but Susan called, and she, Dad, and Wayne were going over to make arrangements at the funeral home. I wanted to be part of everything, and I went over too. I thought the funeral director was quite flippant. He might deal with death all the time, but this was our mother and wife, and I thought he should've been a lot more respectful. I think Susan might have written them a note about it a week or so later, when we were done with the funeral. The arrangements didn't take long because Mom and Dad had already done most all of it years before—that and the fact that the funeral director was in a hurry to get to another funeral!

That evening our children, grandchildren, Dad, Susan, Wayne, and Karen all came over. We ordered pizza. I just wanted to have everyone around. I think Mom must've been close by, showing us to all her family that had passed on years before. It was good to have everyone close. My first counselor in the Relief Society brought over some dinner, but there was just enough for Jack and me. That was the only meal Jack and I got from our ward—not a plate of cookies or anything else. I've always felt bad about that.

During the evening, while I was sitting in my rocking chair in the little family room, Abbie came over to sit with me. She had made a blue beaded bracelet that said "I (heart) GG." She was crying and said "I miss her, Grandma." I told her that I missed her, too, and that we would put the bracelet in her hands when we saw her at the viewing and that she would be buried with it.

I don't remember much about Saturday. I think I went shopping for a new dress to wear to the viewing and funeral. I remember praying that I could find something fast. I stopped off at Penney's and found something right away. I always have a hard time finding clothes to fit, so I felt like that was a little miracle in my behalf.

Sunday was stake conference. We went and had many people come up to me and give me their condolences. It was hard. If I remember correctly, the closing song was "Families Can Be Together Forever."

Monday evening was the viewing at the Valley View funeral home. Susan and I went over in the early afternoon to get Mom dressed. Susan was pretty nervous about it, but I really wasn't. I just kind of floated through that whole weekend and through the funeral. I figured Mom couldn't look any worse than she did when she died, so I wasn't worried about that. We had the funeral director put her garments on her, and then he invited us into the room to dress her in her temple clothes, fix her hair, and put on her makeup. We even put on her perfume—Enjoli.

Susan had forgotten Mom's temple robe and apron, so while she was gone I put a little pair of pearl earrings in her ears. When we were done she looked just beautiful. I thought she looked regal. Dad and Wayne came, and we stayed with Mom for a little while longer and then went home to get ready for the viewing. We came back a little early to set up a "memorial" table. We had gathered pictures and things that were meaningful to Mom and displayed them. I think she would've liked what we did.

Many people came, and we had lots of flowers. When Rebekah, Rob, and the kids came, Abbie and I went up to GG, and we put the little blue bracelet in her hands. I know Mom would've loved that.

The next day we went up to Rigby, Idaho, for the funeral. I kept thinking about how strange it was that all of us were on the road to Rigby, and Mom was in the funeral hearse going up too. She had wanted to go back up to visit her friends but was never able to go the last few years. Now she was going up for the last time. We didn't go in a caravan, but we kept track of each other's whereabouts on our cell phones. When we got there, Mom was already there. Susan and I sat up the memorial table again. Matt and Yvonne were there. It was the first time Matt had seen his grandma. I wanted to be there for him for that. Jack's mother and two of his sisters were there too. It was good to see them. Lots of Mom and Dad's friends came, and it was nice to see them.

When the viewing before the funeral was over, Susan and I put on Mom's veil. Susan put it on and I tied it. We all said our last goodbye. I kissed Mom on her forehead, where I'd kissed her so many times. Dad came forward and pulled the veil down over her face, and the lid was closed on her casket. That was the last we saw of our dear wife and mother.

The chapel was about half full of family and friends. Mom was always afraid no one would come to her funeral—especially since they had moved from Rigby several years before. The funeral went just as she had outlined years before. Rebekah gave the life sketch, which we had worked on in the days before. I had typed it up and added to it, then printed it out after Rebekah had made any changes she wanted to make. Susan had to lead the music because there wasn't anyone else to do it. I didn't think that I'd be able to sing the songs that Mom had chosen, but I was actually able to. She wanted "I Stand All Amazed" and "The Lord is My Shepherd." I was able to sing them there because I felt like it was a tribute to Mom, but the next time we sang "I Stand All Amazed" in sacrament meeting, I couldn't sing it at all.

After the funeral we went out to the cemetery, and Jack dedicated the grave. We stood around for a little while, and those that wanted flowers for a remembrance took them. The ones I took are still hanging on the corner of the curtain by my kitchen window. Afterwards, Mom and Dad's old Rigby ward provided dinner for us. It tasted wonderful. It was good to have the whole family together. Even Susan's ex-husband, Don Hales, came from Flagstaff, Arizona, which I thought was nice. It was the first time I had spoken or seen him since their divorce. I know Mom was happy that we had sort of mended fences and were on speaking terms again.

After the dinner, we waited for Rebekah and Yvonne to feed their babies, and then we said goodbye to Matt and Yvonne and made the trip back down to Utah.

This has been a kind of "matter of fact" rendition, but it really wasn't while it was happening. Even though it was hard to go through those last few years, I always felt like it was an honor and a privilege to be there for Mom. I always told her that now it was my turn to take care of her because she had done such a wonderful job of taking care of me for so many years. The last several months of her life, when I helped her with her showers and other personal care things, she could never thank me enough. Sometimes she felt humiliated at having to have someone do for her what she couldn't do for herself anymore. I always tried to make her feel like it was okay and that I was happy to be there to help her and Dad. Even though I would never wish her back to the life she led the last few years, I sometimes miss not being able to go down and bring her glasses of ice, or help her into bed at night, with a few more pieces of ice before I left.

I know that she isn't far away. I always thought that she would come back and let me know she was close—like her mother did for her when she died. Mom hasn't done that yet, but I know she's nearby. Many times at night before I go to sleep, or when I'm here at home alone, I say, "Where are you Mom? What are you doing?" For years she did genealogy, and for about a year I was doing it too. Back in the mid '80s we looked for my fourth great-grandparents, John Setterington and Alice Burbidge, and were never able to find anything about them—even with Mom hiring a professional researcher for awhile. About six months after Mom passed away, I started taking a family history class at church. One day I was at the computer and decided to "Google" John Setterington and Alice Burbidge. I found a whole site that had their names and much of the genealogy that Mom had in her records. One area of this site had an Elizabeth Burbidge that was married to John Setterington. I took notes and had a feeling that those were my fourth great-grandparents. There was an email address of the person that had submitted the information. I emailed him and shortly received a reply. He was actually a distant cousin, and Mom and Dad had met with him years before when he lived in eastern Canada. His name is George Setterington. To make a long story short, Alice's name was really Elizabeth (her mother's name was Alice), and not only did he have all of hers and John's information, but he had gone back two more generations! I know now the answers to my questions—Where are you, Mom? And what are you doing? She's right here close, and she's letting me know how to find the genealogy information that is needed to have the temple work done for all these ancestors. She's clear of mind and strong of body, and she's busy doing what needs to be done. She's no longer in her old, frail body. She's healthy and strong again.

POEM OUR DAD WROTE FOR MOM
IN THEIR LATER YEARS

You've asked me now for quite awhile
To write a line or two,
So I'll take the time on Mother's Day
To write a verse for you.

God had a special purpose
When He created mothers
Oh, how many times I've told you
You tower above the others.

He gave you special things to do
That no other woman can.
He gave you strength to care for me,
A stubborn mortal man.

Whose head seems hard as granite,
Who seems to never bend,
But this man, your husband
Will love you till the end.

Maybe we're just gypsies.
We've tramped around a bit,
But in the lap of luxury
We've not been blessed to sit.

But wealth isn't all mere money,
Just think of our friends so dear,

146

The pleasures we've had together
That have lasted through the years.

There isn't time or paper enough,
It would take me all my life
To put into mere words and verse
My love for you, my wife.

Now to wind this poem up, my dear,
You're the greatest wife and mother;
You've raised your three and stuck with me,
For me there is no other.

www.ingramcontent.com/pod-product-compliance
Lightning Source LLC
Chambersburg PA
CBHW061727020426

42331CB00006B/1140